Praise for

"Whenever you sit down to write a book about a championship team several words emerge that can universally apply to all of them—determination, sacrifice, commitment, focus, shared goals, and hard work are but a few. Doug Brunk has captured these words and even more in this book about one of Kentucky's greatest teams, the 1977–1978 National Champion Wildcats. If you are a part of the Big Blue Nation or just a basketball fan, you will enjoy the anecdotes and stories of a team that had tremendous pressure on them to win the national title. Their journey through the season culminating with a win over Duke in the championship game gives you a good historical perspective and is great reading."
—*Larry Conley,* member of Kentucky's 1966 national runner-up team known as "Rupp's Runts," and former college basketball broadcaster

"Kentucky's 1978 national championship season has been described as a season without celebration. But Doug Brunk's book *Forty Minutes to Glory* paints a different picture of a group of talented players who dedicated themselves to achieving a special goal before the season ever started. There is a reason Kentucky teams are so beloved by their passionate fan base and why their fans can quote you chapter and verse on the great moments in the program's story. The names of Kyle Macy, Rick Robey, Goose Givens, Mike Phillips, James Lee, and Jay Shidler will always be beloved by the Big Blue Nation for their talent and work ethic. Brunk does a great job bringing out their personalities and their resolve to reach Olympian heights under Joe B. Hall, who coached the Cats' first national title since 1958 and put the Cats back in their rightful place as the No. 1 program in college basketball. After reading this book, it's hard not to fall in love with them."
—*Dick "Hoops" Weiss,* former college basketball writer for the *Philadelphia Daily News* and *New York Daily News* and member of the US Basketball Writers Association Hall of Fame

"What a great read for all Kentucky and basketball fans, young and old, everywhere. I was in St. Louis for the semifinals and there the

day of the finals, and the atmosphere was electric. The dramatic accounts from the players are riveting, and the pressures they all felt only served to heighten the drama of the game so aptly described in this book. Expectations of Kentucky winning the championship were huge, but expectations are not results. You have to play the game, and play the game they did. Now, Jack Givens, James Lee, Rick Robey, Mike Phillips, Truman Claytor, and Dwane Casey are legends. There were some great additions to that team, but none so valuable as Kyle Macy—one of the best floor generals in UK history. Kentucky had everything. Coaching, size, speed, the best bench in the country, toughness, shooting, defense, and more shooting. They had an abundance of everything, including a killer instinct. They looked like choirboys and played like wildcats!"
—*Reggie Warford,* point guard for the University of Kentucky men's basketball team, 1972–1976

"I really enjoyed this book on the 1978 NCAA champs—a team that seemed to be misunderstood in many ways. *Forty Minutes to Glory* shines a different light on their march to the championship. They were a terrific team coached by the only man who could have gotten them to the finish line!"
—*Mike Pratt,* forward for the University of Kentucky men's basketball team, 1967–1970, and broadcast analyst for the UK Radio Network

"What a great book! The author puts you in the team huddle with the 1978 National Champs. The UK basketball nostalgia and insights are entertaining. Who knew this team would be so close but have multiple altercations during their practices!"
—*Roger Harden,* point guard for the University of Kentucky men's basketball team, 1982–1986

"What a great book for all Wildcat fans. A fun and fast read for all ages, it contains detailed insights and takes you behind the scenes of a historic season!"
—*Jim Master,* shooting guard for the University of Kentucky men's basketball team, 1980–1984

Forty Minutes to Glory

FORTY MINUTES TO
GLORY

*Inside the Kentucky Wildcats'
1978 Championship Season*

Doug Brunk

Forewords by
Larry Vaught and Tom Leach

Featuring accounts by
Jack Givens, Joe B. Hall, and Others

Copyright © 2018 by The University Press of Kentucky

Scholarly publisher for the Commonwealth,
serving Bellarmine University, Berea College, Centre College of Kentucky,
Eastern Kentucky University, The Filson Historical Society, Georgetown
College, Kentucky Historical Society, Kentucky State University, Morehead
State University, Murray State University, Northern Kentucky University,
Transylvania University, University of Kentucky, University of Louisville,
and Western Kentucky University.
All rights reserved.

Editorial and Sales Offices: The University Press of Kentucky
663 South Limestone Street, Lexington, Kentucky 40508-4008
www.kentuckypress.com

Cataloging-in-Publication data is available from the Library of Congress.

ISBN 978-0-8131-7520-1 (paperback : alk. paper)
ISBN 978-0-8131-7522-5 (epub)
ISBN 978-0-8131-7521-8 (pdf)

This book is printed on acid-free paper meeting
the requirements of the American National Standard
for Permanence in Paper for Printed Library Materials.

Manufactured in the United States of America.

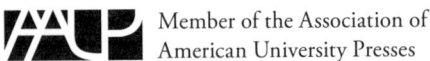 Member of the Association of
American University Presses

This book is dedicated to the 1977–1978
University of Kentucky Wildcats
men's basketball team.

If you're number one, boy, you've got to work harder than anyone else because it's harder to stay there than it is to get there.

—Bill Keightley, longtime equipment manager for the University of Kentucky men's basketball program

Contents

Foreword xiii
  Larry Vaught
Foreword xix
  Tom Leach
Author's Note xxii
Introduction 1
1. The Tone Is Set 9
2. Grueling Practices 23
3. Farewell to Rupp 37
4. Christening Wildcat Lodge 55
5. A Cold Snap and a Loss 65
6. Navigating the "Pressure Cooker" 75
7. Tourney Time 89
8. Meet Me in St. Louis 97
9. Forty Minutes to Glory 107
10. Extraordinary Reception 125
11. Beyond the Title 135
12. A Shackle-Breaking Experience 147
    Joe B. Hall

13. The Art of Being Prepared   151
    Rob Bolton
14. A Lesson in the Value of Hard Work   155
    Mike Murphy
15. A Storybook Ending   161
    Jack Givens

Acknowledgments   165

Appendix 1. St. Louis and Five Smooth Stones   169
    Rev. David N. Blondell

Appendix 2. Senate Resolution 427: A Commendation for the Wildcats   173

About the Author   177

Notes   179

Index   185

Foreword

Ask Rick Robey about his fondest memory of Kentucky's 1978 national championship season and he doesn't hesitate to give an answer.

"The fondest memory was when we finally won it," said Robey, who came to the University of Kentucky (UK) from Louisiana and now lives in Louisville. "We set our goals other years and got close. Going into that season ranked as the top team in the country—and the pressure that put on us because everybody expected us to do it—was pretty intense. When the buzzer went off [in the championship game against Duke], it was a big relief. It was such a close-knit group of guys and even to this day still is. We all stay in touch. It was just fun and something you never forget."

Kentucky's 94–88 victory over Duke in the title game climaxed a miraculous season for the Wildcats. The UK seniors had lost in the 1975 title game, won the National Invitational Tournament (NIT) in 1976, and lost in the regional finals to North Carolina in 1977. But the addition of Purdue-transfer Kyle Macy at point guard to go with seniors Robey, Mike Phillips, Jack Givens, and James Lee made the Cats the darlings of the Bluegrass.

Givens went out with one of the most memorable performances in UK history. He hit 18 of 27 shots from the field and had 41 points. Kentucky Coach Joe B. Hall figured out where the hole was in Duke's zone defense. UK kept feeding Givens, and he just kept making shots. Even now, Givens admits he could not imagine a better way to end his career. "There was no finer way to go out," Givens said. "We had worked so hard to get that title, and we finally got it. We knew not only what it meant to us, but to people across the state. Even today I still have people wanting to talk to me about the game or that season. It never gets old."

Doug Brunk's book takes an inside look at the 1977–1978 Kentucky men's basketball campaign with stories and anecdotes from players that bring the season back to life. Even though I covered that team as a young sports reporter and was in St. Louis when UK won, Brunk has gathered stories and information about that season that I did not know, ranging from the time James Lee quit the team for an afternoon to Kyle Macy's babysitting for UK radio color analyst Ralph Hacker to Scott Courts's having a girl on their first date tell him his first step on the hardwood was not quick enough.

That season was full of stories, too. One of UK's two losses was 95–94 at Louisiana State University (LSU) in mid-February when the Tigers had all five starters foul out and still won. A month earlier, UK had beaten LSU 96–76 in Rupp Arena, and after that game LSU Coach Dale Brown charged that UK was "brutalizing" college basketball with its physical play and went on a tirade that touched on murder, rape, epilepsy, Sirhan Sirhan, and a sportswriter's sex habits. "Yet when we beat Kentucky, there was Joe Hall congratulating me after what I had said about his team," Brown said. "That was a classy thing to do, and that team was so good. I really don't think that team gets the credit it deserves for how good it was."

How physical was that Kentucky team that featured Robey and Phillips, who were nicknamed the "Twin Towers" for their six-foot, ten-inch frames, as well as the muscular, six-foot, five-inch Lee? "If Mike got upset, somebody was going to get hurt," Givens laughed and said. "I stopped telling James to stop hurting people. It was not always on purpose, but he would hurt people, too. If I had a guy giving me trouble, I just ran him off a screen that Mike or James set, and that was usually it."

Robey took pride in the physical reputation Kentucky had. He said anyone who thought games were physical should have seen practices—and Brunk includes detailed accounts in the book to verify that. "Any time you had the size we had—even the backup guys like LaVon Williams and Freddie Cowan—and get that many big guys inside, you have a tendency to be physical. Then James and Mike and myself, that was our style of play," Robey said. "It was kind of the first time in the college game that two 6-foot, 10-inch guys played together." He noted that UK's "bigs" knew to take it easy on the smaller guards in practice. "We didn't pick on them like real opponents," he said. "We did not want to try to hurt Macy. We needed him for games."

Everyone has their special memories of that season, starting with the preseason scrimmages across the state that had yet to be banned by the NCAA. Fans turned out en masse to see their beloved Wildcats. Perhaps my best memory is of making the trek from Danville to Lexington in treacherous conditions to watch UK play. The month of January 1978 was frigid and snowy. Blizzard conditions closed highways, and schools were out most of the month. Yet a couple of times I drove with a friend, current Boyle County, Kentucky, Judge-Executive Harold McKinney, in his Volkswagen to games when we could see no farther than three cars ahead of us on the thirty-five-mile drive to Lexington. But guess what? Once we got to Rupp Arena, close to twenty thousand UK fans were there to watch the eventual national champions play and thought it was more than worth the effort it took to get to the game.

"That is what Kentucky basketball is all about," Robey said. "It's just like [Big Blue] Madness now gets twenty-three thousand fans to watch what isn't even a real practice. After our senior year we did a barnstorming tour, and every city we went into just had great fans. It is what makes Kentucky basketball. It's not the players; it's the fans. That will never change and why, as crazy as it sounds, we knew people would be there no matter how much it snowed, and we owed it to them to play our very best every game, but especially in those games."

There's a great story in the book about the late Bill Keightley and his devotion to the UK basketball program. He actually lived at Memorial Coliseum for a week during the blizzard conditions. I'll also never forget the most daring coaching move I've ever seen by a UK coach. In the NCAA Tournament opener in Knoxville against underdog Florida State, Kentucky trailed 39–32 at halftime. Coach Hall was furious, and it showed as he left the court. He stunned everyone by benching starters Robey, Givens, and Truman Claytor to start the second half and went with Macy, Mike Phillips, and reserves LaVon Williams, Fred Cowan, and Dwane Casey. If UK had lost, fans would never have forgiven Coach Hall. He kept the three starters on the bench until midway of the half, and once they returned, UK went on a 14–0 run and won 85–76. Coach Brown says it still ranks as one of the most courageous coaching moves he's seen. "I gave Joe a hard time, but he never got the credit he deserved," he said.

Two games later, UK played Michigan State, which had a relatively unknown player—Earvin "Magic" Johnson. The Spartans led 27–22 at halftime before Coach Hall and Assistant Coach Leonard Hamilton devised a play just before the second half started to enable Robey to set screens to free Macy for shots against the 2–3 zone. It worked, as Macy hit key shots and free throws in the second half to secure UK's 52–49 win. That still ranks as one of the most intense games I've ever seen because every possession was so precious. "I don't think anyone for Kentucky involved in that game will ever forget it," Macy said. "That was one of the special games in a special season."

The biggest misconception about that season was that UK had no fun. Coach Hall did say it had been a "season of no celebration" at the Final Four because of UK's goal to win the title. But anyone who knew the players on that team realizes it was a fun-loving group that understood how to enjoy time away from basketball when they had it. "Everybody thought we were real serious, but believe me this was a group of guys that did a lot off the floor and on the floor to have fun," Robey said. "We knew our strengths and weaknesses. That's why we had the type of team we had. Winning was our number one priority. However, that did not mean we never had fun during the season. There were a lot of good times."

Now the players have a good time speculating with fans on where they rank among the all-time best teams at Kentucky. Most fans rank either the 1996 team that won the title for Coach Rick Pitino or the 2012 team that won for Coach John Calipari as the best and most talented. "Personally, I would not want to play against that team that went 38–0 before losing to Wisconsin in the Final Four," said Givens, referring to the 2014–2015 squad. "That team had really good size, experience, quickness. I would say my 1978 team might not beat that team."

He admitted teammates might not agree. "If you would ask Kyle or Rick, they would say we would kill that team—or any other UK team," Givens said. "I am not sure. That team had some players. But I know our group would have probably welcomed that kind of challenge. We liked that."

Givens is glad that Coach Calipari has put "Kentucky basketball back in its rightful place" as the number one program in the country. "I don't care who you watch or listen to, if you talk college basketball—good or bad—the first team everybody wants to talk about is Kentucky," Givens said.

Macy still lives in Lexington and understands that well. Fans still stop him to ask for autographs or pictures.

"Every day I have somebody say something to me about that team or season," Robey said. "I get stuff in the mail at least four or five times a week from people wanting things signed. It is amazing what that team meant to so many people."

It's also why this book is a must-read for older UK fans because of the new information they may learn about that team or the chance just to relive the season. For younger fans, it's a history lesson about a team and season that was special from start to finish.

Larry Vaught
Danville, Kentucky

Foreword

When Coach Joe B. Hall, on the eve of the national title game against Duke, said, "This has been a season without celebration for us," some writers jumped on the bandwagon of writing about the crazy Kentucky fans who demanded nothing less than a title from their teams and how that took the fun out of the game for the players. But if you talk to the players on that team, the reason they were not celebrating any achievements along the way was because of their singular focus, like an Olympic athlete on a four-year pursuit of a gold medal.

It was a senior-dominated group of players that knew this was their last chance to get the championship that had eluded them. As freshmen, they surely felt they had won the title when they upset undefeated and top-ranked Indiana in the Mideast Regional Final. But they fell short in the finale, to a UCLA squad motivated by the knowledge that it was the last game for legendary coach John Wooden. As juniors, Jack Givens, James Lee, Rick Robey, and Mike Phillips were the core of a team that felt it was good enough to get the ring, only to fall behind North Carolina in an East Regional Final and see the Tar Heels use their vaunted "four corners" offense to secure the victory.

As seniors, Givens, Lee, Robey, and Phillips led the team to a number-one ranking, and despite an overpowering campaign that saw them slip up only twice, that foursome knew nothing less than a championship would satisfy them. Add in a coach who was following in the footsteps of a legend, and it's easy to see why that team's laser focus on a goal was mistaken for a crippling form of pressure.

Replacing Larry Johnson at guard was the major challenge coming into the 1978 season, but Hall knew he had an ace in the hole when it came to that task because he had Purdue-transfer Kyle Macy coming off a redshirt year to take the reins at the point. With Truman Claytor and Jay Shidler, the Cats had two long-range shooters to keep the pressure off the big men in the paint, and in the years that followed, everyone would also come to understand just how good some of the players farther down the bench in 1978 really were. It was a deep roster but with players willing to sacrifice for the good of the team.

The best example of the 1978 team's mindset comes from a story Coach Hall tells about the night before the title game against the Cinderella team from Duke in St. Louis. Hall suggested to the players that they take a break and go see a movie as a team. Robey countered by saying the players wanted to watch the tape of Duke's semifinal win over Notre Dame instead.

On game night, "Goose" Givens turned in one of the best performances in the history of the NCAA Tournament, torching Duke's 2–3 zone time and time again for 41 points, as the Wildcats scored a 94–88 victory. "The Goose Was Golden" was the headline on the cover of the next edition of *Sports Illustrated*.

Any Wildcat fan who ventured out to what was then known as Bluegrass Field to welcome home the 1978 national championship basketball team can fondly recall the scene as vividly today as when it occurred. Cars were parked along the sides of roads leading to the airport, as the parking lots could not handle the volume of traffic, and the scene in the airport's lobby when the team arrived provided one of the great pictures in UK's storied basketball history.

For Big Blue fans, it was a party twenty years in the making, since that's how long it had been since the last title. Near misses in 1966 and 1975 didn't hurt quite so much when basking in the joy of the Wildcats' claiming the school's fifth national title. And the championship served to cement the legacy of Hall—and one would be hard-pressed to find a coach who did a better job of following a legend.

If you were along for that memorable ride, you'll enjoy reliving the journey through the recollections of players, coaches, and others associated with the team. And if you're a UK fan of a younger age, then consider it a necessary history lesson about one of the greatest Kentucky teams ever.

Tom Leach
"The Voice of the Wildcats"
Lexington, Kentucky

Author's Note

Unless otherwise noted, direct quotes in this book were based on interviews I conducted between November 2015 and November 2016 with former coaches, players, managers, support staff, and other individuals who were close to the 1977–1978 University of Kentucky Wildcats men's basketball team. Some of the interviews took place in person, but most were conducted by telephone. I asked each source the same general set of questions, and others based on that person's unique contributions to the team.

This book also includes stand-alone first-person essays from four sources interviewed for this book—Coach Joe B. Hall, Rob Bolton, Mike Murphy, and Jack Givens. I hope their valuable contributions enrich the reader's experience and provide unique insights of interest to Kentucky fans.

Mindful of the challenges in asking sources to remember specific details from four decades ago, in many cases I double-checked quotes with interviewees to corroborate stories and recollections.

Introduction

Jack "Goose" Givens. Rick Robey. Mike Phillips. James Lee. Battle-tested as underclassmen, these four seniors who entered the 1977–1978 University of Kentucky men's basketball season had come close to bringing home a fifth National Collegiate Athletic Association (NCAA) Division I crown to Lexington, but they couldn't catch a break. In 1975 they lost to the UCLA Bruins 92–85 in the NCAA National Championship game. In 1976 they failed to qualify for the NCAA Tournament due to losing ten games that season, but prevailed as champions in the National Invitational Tournament with a 71–67 win over the University of North Carolina (UNC) Charlotte 49ers. In 1977, Kentucky lost 79–72 to the UNC Tar Heels in the NCAA East Regional Finals, with the winner advancing to the Final Four.[1]

The 1977–1978 Wildcat squad would be different. It was deep in every position, and playing the seasoned Robey and Phillips together, who both had six-foot, ten-inch frames, created a matchup nightmare for opponents. Then there was the ever-steady sophomore guard Kyle Macy, a transfer from Purdue University, who led the team in free-throw shooting that year with a clip of 89 percent, a skill that would prove instrumental in the outcome of a few games that season. As longtime Assistant Coach Dick Parsons put it, "the right ingredients" were in place for success that season. "Boy, we had good shooters," he said of the team, which made 54 percent of its field goals during the campaign. "We were shooting in the 60 percent range sometimes. It was a unique team. We didn't have another one quite like it when I was there."

A deep-seated resolve to win an NCAA Championship title would ultimately define this team. The genesis of that determination stemmed from the prior season's loss to North Carolina in the East Regional Finals. Truman Claytor, a junior guard at the time, characterized that loss as "devastating" to Givens, Robey, Phillips, and Lee in particular. "It was devastating to me, too, because I wanted so badly to win the national championship," he said. "We were on our way back to Lexington on the plane, and those guys said, 'This is what we need to do. Everyone needs to stay in Lexington throughout the summer, lift weights, play every day, and stay together, and work toward that one common goal: to win the NCAA [championship],' because we didn't want to have that feeling again: getting so close."

The 1977–1978 Wildcats competed during an era of college basketball almost unrecognizable to the one that exists today. Back then, most college basketball players stayed in school for four years. There was no shot clock, no three-point shot, no ESPN, no Internet, no cell phones, no elaborate press conferences announcing a high school recruit's college choice; and the NCAA Men's Basketball Tournament was limited to thirty-two teams, compared with the sixty-eight who are invited to the "Big Dance" in this day and age. "Unfortunately, because it was 1978 and not 1979, a lot of people across the country don't know how good this team really was," Macy added. "The following year you had ESPN and all the media exposure of the Larry Bird and Magic Johnson finals game.[2] Had that been a year later, then I think everybody would have appreciated this team for how good it really was: no weaknesses, the toughness, the experience, the focus, and the versatility." Not only that,

NCAA coaches during this span of play were generally more deliberate in working freshmen into their rotations.[3] "Young guys came in, fell in line, appreciated the older players, and did what they were told to do," observed six-foot, two-inch guard Chris Gettelfinger, a Knoxville, Tennessee, native who earned a spot as a freshman walk-on for the Wildcats in 1977. "Now, they come in as freshmen knowing they're one-and-done, so it's a whole different thing."

The roster of this team included six players who had earned "Mr. Basketball" titles as high school seniors, each in different states: Givens (Kentucky), Macy (Indiana), Phillips (Ohio), Robey (Louisiana), Jay Shidler (Illinois), and Denver native LaVon Williams (so honored at the time by the "Four Corners" states of Arizona, Colorado, New Mexico, and Utah). This team was also the first in Wildcat history to earn a national championship with Rupp Arena as its home court, a feat replicated by only three others: the Rick Pitino–led squad that defeated Syracuse 76–67 in 1996, the Tubby Smith–led team that beat Utah 78–69 in 1998, and the John Calipari–led squad that defeated Kansas 67–59 in 2012. Although Rupp Arena opened in 1976, Don Sullivan, who was head student manager for the 1977–1978 Wildcats, said that it took a while for the twenty-three thousand–seat facility to feel like home court. "Now they have all blue seating in there, but at that time the seats were colored in red, yellow, and orange," Sullivan said. In his opinion, Kentucky's victory in the 1978 NCAA Men's Basketball Championship triggered a shift in how the venue was perceived. "It got the attention of the Lexington Center people in saying, 'This is what your facility is: it is a UK facility,'" he said.

While highlights from certain games during the 1977–1978 season are included in this book, *Forty Minutes to Glory* draws from the personal anecdotes and recollections of sources interviewed for this project to emphasize what was going on behind the scenes. For example, the simmering resolve the incoming seniors had to win the national championship was vocalized during the first official team meeting of the season, which took place in September 1977, just off the training room in Memorial Coliseum. When Coach Hall asked the team what it wanted to accomplish that year, cocaptain and senior center Rick Robey stood up and said, "Coach, I think I speak for everybody in the room when I say nothing less than the national championship is going to be acceptable for this team. That's what we want." After hearing this, "my eyes got big," recalled then twenty-three-year-old Joe Dean Jr. who was beginning his first season as an assistant coach for the Wildcats. "I thought, 'Wow.'"

Givens, the team's cocaptain, was equally fired up. "The good thing is, all the young guys got on board very quickly with what we said in that meeting," he said. "It was not a problem getting everybody to understand what it was going to take for us to get done what we wanted to get done."

Sports media from the time referred to UK's 1977–1978 campaign as "The Season of No Celebration" due to the players' laser focus on their resolve to win a national title, coupled with Coach Joe B. Hall's reputation as a taskmaster and a disciplinarian. By all accounts, this squad was serious-minded, almost businesslike in its quest to bring a fifth NCAA Championship to Lexington. "We were graced by having great spiritual and moral leaders on this team," freshman center Scott Courts said. "We were driven by the force of discipline, morality, and spirit. There was no question about that; it was almost a divine mission. There wasn't anyone on that team that didn't conduct themselves within those boundaries."

Longtime UK Radio Network broadcaster Ralph Hacker underscored the role Coach Hall played in the ultimate success of this team. "They had a tremendous amount of talent, but you had to have somebody who channeled that talent," Hacker observed. "I think Joe B. was the driving force to harness all those people, bring them together, and put them right down the path. Beyond that, you

From left, Kentucky seniors James Lee, Rick Robey, Mike Phillips, and Jack Givens began the 1977–1978 season determined to end their collegiate careers as national champions. (Courtesy of the *Lexington Herald-Leader*. Photo by David Perry.)

had Macy, a guy who could lead anybody on a basketball court. He proved that year after year since high school. Then you had some unique things that came along and fell in place as the year went along, like the further development of Jack Givens, or the part that Jay Shidler and Rick Robey played. All of those guys played a role."

Assistant Coach Leonard Hamilton remarked about how well the players reacted to Coach Hall's demands. "The harder he pushed them, the better they responded," he said. "During those moments when you're really challenged and you can get your feelings hurt, these guys responded in a mature way. Those were the real reasons why we were able to be successful. This team had that elusive thing called 'it' that makes the difference between good and great teams."

This season was marked by several intriguing storylines besides a remarkable 30–2 record, with Kentucky ranked number one in Associated Press polls for all but four weeks of regular-season play, and never falling below number three. For one, the 1978 NCAA Championship marked the first basketball crown for UK in twenty years and the first to be guided by someone other than Coach Adolph Rupp, who led teams to four NCAA Championships during his forty-two-year tenure. Ironically, Coach Rupp, a native of Halstead, Kansas, passed away from cancer on December 11, 1977, when the Wildcats were in Lawrence, Kansas, for a matchup against the Jayhawks—for whom Rupp had played in the 1920s under Coach Forrest "Phog" Allen. Later that same month, the Kentucky players moved into Wildcat Lodge, a new freestanding dorm for basketball players that featured individual rooms and bathrooms, and a basement with a pool table, a ping-pong table, two pinball machines, and a large-screen television set. Coach Hall helped raise money for the facility, which was paid for by donations from boosters and leaders in the state's coal-mining industry. "It was something special, and I think it probably gave the players a sense of appreciation, that Kentucky basketball really was a highly valued group and team that so many people would put so much into a facility for them to live in," Joe Dean Jr. observed. "I think it added to the attitude of that team as we were going through that year."

The team physician, Dr. V. A. Jackson, and his wife, Marie, a nurse, moved in with the team and assumed a role as houseparents—and not without sacrifice. They sold a newly built home, designed to their own specifications, for the opportunity to serve in this capacity. "I wanted to instill in them the good things: going to church and being a good guy," recalled Marie Jackson, who on Sundays often brought players to Buck Run Baptist Church in Frankfort, Kentucky, and other churches to speak or to share their testimony. "These were really good guys."

Forty Minutes to Glory includes other behind-the-scenes anecdotes for UK basketball fans, such as the time James Lee quit the team for an afternoon and how Assistant Coach Dick Parsons admonished an NCAA official in the Checkerdome for not having enough courtside chairs for the team the night of the championship game. This book also contains first-person essays from Coach Hall, Givens, and former assistant student managers Rob Bolton and Mike Murphy, who shared their perspectives on what made this team so special.

Earning the 1978 NCAA crown was bittersweet for one Wildcat. The father of Scott Courts died from a heart attack in Minnesota just two days before the Final Four at the Checkerdome in St. Louis, Missouri. "I remember a mass of people and the pressure and the mania and the chaos," said Courts, who arrived by plane in St. Louis hours before the tip-off of the title game. "I was in shock. I was grieving the loss of my father. It was so strange to have the lowest point of your life and then you're getting ready to experience the highest point in your life, and to experience a level of glory that you know you'll never experience again. You don't know that at [age] eighteen, but that was the fact."

Nearly four decades have passed since this squad cut down the nets in St. Louis, but without fail every person interviewed for this book—from players to coaches to managers and other support staff—expressed how the achievement grows more special with each passing year. "As time goes by, I still feel like, 'Wow. What an accomplishment,' because I see year after year how hard it is to win a national championship," said Truman Claytor, who was born in Ashland, Kentucky. "I cherish it even more to this day, forty years later, winning a national title. Winning it at Kentucky? There's nothing like it. You're always going to be remembered for winning the national title in the great tradition of Kentucky basketball that never goes away."

1

The Tone Is Set

As the excitement of a new semester unfolded on the campus of the University of Kentucky in September 1977, players, coaches, and support staff for the 1977–1978 men's basketball team gathered in a room in Memorial Coliseum for the first time.

Four team members entered the season as seniors: six-foot, four-inch forward and cocaptain Jack Givens of Lexington, Kentucky; six-foot, ten-inch forward-center and cocaptain Rick Robey of New Orleans, Louisiana; six-foot, ten-inch center Mike Phillips of Akron, Ohio; and six-foot, five-inch forward James Lee, also of Lexington. This foursome enjoyed deep college basketball tournament runs as underclassmen but had fallen short of an NCAA crown year after year, experiences that intensified their desire to finish their collegiate careers as national champions. It started their freshman year with a matchup against UCLA in the NCAA National Championship game in San Diego, California, on March 31, 1975. After the Bruins edged out Louisville in overtime at the national semifinals on March 29, UCLA Coach John Wooden announced his intent to retire after the title game, a development that added intrigue to the event, if not a certain shrewdness. "I knew right then that would be a big influence on the game," Coach Joe B. Hall told a reporter in 2010.[1]

Wooden used only six players in the game, but it was enough to guide his team to a 92–85 victory over Kentucky—the tenth UCLA national title in his twenty-seven-year career as the "Wizard of Westwood." Senior Wildcat forward Kevin Grevey finished his career by pouring in 34 points, senior center Bob Guyette added 16, and senior guard Mike Flynn chipped in 10. Combined, Robey, Givens, Phillips, and Lee scored just 16 points. Losing that game "really hurt, because we had a chance to win it," Coach Hall recalled. "We should have; we were good enough to have won it." Assistant Coach Leonard Hamilton said that the 1975 Wildcats "were challenged mentally and emotionally by the enormous amount of hype caused by the fact that it was Wooden's last game. There were a lot of things I thought put some added pressure on our team." As a result of the experience gained in that game, then-freshmen Givens, Robey, Phillips, and Lee "drew wisdom from how we responded to that championship game," Hamilton said. "I just felt that they understood the mindset we had to be in, and we were not going to allow that moment to slip away."

As sophomores, this foursome and their teammates failed to qualify for the NCAA Tournament due to losing ten games—and Robey was out for much of the season with a knee injury—but they won their final ten games of the year, including a 71–67 victory over the UNC Charlotte 49ers in the National Invitational Tournament (NIT) Championship game in New York City on March 21, 1976. Phillips and junior guard Larry Johnson led the Wildcats by scoring 16 points apiece. "I've always thought that win laid the foundation for the team two years later to win the NCAA National Championship," said Ralph Hacker, who was the late Cawood Ledford's broadcast partner on the UK Radio Network before becoming the play-by-play announcer in 1992.[2] "It showed them what they could do."

From left, Dick Parsons and Joe B. Hall not only played for Adolph Rupp, they served on his coaching staff. Here they pose with Coach Rupp and fellow assistant coach Gale Catlett (far right) during the 1971–1972 season. When Hall succeeded Rupp as UK's head coach the following season, Parsons joined his staff. (Courtesy of the University of Kentucky Archives.)

According to Coach Hall, not everyone on the team was thrilled about playing in the NIT. In fact, some of the players intimated that they preferred to spend spring break in Florida with friends rather than travel to New York City to keep their hoops season rolling. One day they approached their coach to ask for a vote.

"I said, 'Fine. What do you want to vote on?'" Coach Hall said.

"They said, 'Well, we want to vote on whether to go to the NIT or not. A lot of us don't want to go.'

"I said, 'You don't know, but we've already had the vote.'

"'What was the outcome?'

"'One to nothing. Get in there and get ready to practice!' We stayed ten days in New York and beat some really good teams."

The next year, this quartet of juniors and their fellow Wildcats looked like national title contenders by earning a 24–3 regular-season record, including a 50-point victory over Texas Christian University, 40-point wins over Vanderbilt and Florida, and a 15-point victory over Indiana in Bloomington. In postseason play, Kentucky advanced to the NCAA East Regional Finals in College Park, Maryland, for a matchup against the North Carolina Tar Heels on March 19, 1977. Despite a 26-point effort from Givens, 15 points from Robey, and 12 from Phillips, North Carolina got the best of Kentucky that day in a 79–72 victory by connecting on 33 of 36 free throws and running its four-corners delay offense near the end of the game. They also outshot the Wildcats from the floor 61 percent to 46 percent. "It was very frustrating," Mike Phillips said of the loss, in a 1977 interview with *The Cats' Pause*.[3] "There's not much you can do about it except to reflect back and not allow it to happen again. In the locker room, it was a pretty dismal scene because everybody was in the frame of mind that we had let each other down, more or less, and let ourselves down." Truman Claytor, a junior guard at the time, characterized that loss as "devastating" to Givens, Robey, Phillips, and Lee in particular. "It was devastating to me, too, because I wanted so badly to win the national championship," he said. "We were on our way back to Lexington on the plane and those guys said, 'This is what we need to do. Everyone needs to stay in Lexington throughout the summer, lift weights, play every day, and stay together, and work toward that one common goal: to win the NCAA [championship],' because we didn't want to have that feeling again: getting so close."

That loss to the Tar Heels made Robey think about how special the next season's Wildcats would be, especially with the anticipated debut of Kyle Macy, a six-foot, three-inch point guard who had redshirted during the 1976–1977 campaign after transferring from Purdue. Named Indiana's "Mr. Basketball" as a high school senior in 1975, Macy had been practicing with the team and preparing for his role as a starting point guard. "I just knew the four of

The Tone Is Set　13

Pictured left to right as freshmen in 1974 are Kentucky players Rick Robey, Dan Hall, James Lee, Jack Givens, and Mike Phillips. (Courtesy of the University of Kentucky Archives.)

us [seniors] were going to mature from the experience that we had our junior year," Robey said. "With Kyle, Truman Claytor, and Jay Shidler, I knew we had the guard position taken care of. We had the right chemistry, and we were all on a mission."

Indeed, the 1977–1978 team would be different. Once everyone gathered in Memorial Coliseum on that September day of 1977, Coach Hall said, "'Gentlemen, we're getting ready to start a new year, a new season,'" recalled Joe Dean Jr., who was starting his first year as an assistant coach for the Wildcats. "'Nothing we've done in the past means anything. It's all about what we're going to do this coming year. What do you guys want to do?'" As if on cue, Dean continued, Robey stood up and said, "'Coach, I think I speak for everybody in the room when I say nothing less than the national championship is going to be acceptable for this team. That's what we want.' My eyes got big. I thought, 'Wow.'"

Lee remembered standing up and saying, "'Coach, you draw up the Xs and Os, and we'll take care of it.' You could see the burden lifted off of him. He knew what he had, and we knew how determined the team was." Lee and the other three seniors "had seen it all, been through it all, and we just weren't going to be denied," he said. "All we fell short of doing is being undefeated. We had learned a great deal from some great teams, so when we became seniors, it was just automatic for us. We knew what we wanted to do, and we were destined to get it."

Dwane Casey, then a junior guard, said that the team's four seniors led by example on and off the court. "They had been there before, so they knew how to play, how to compete, how to prepare, how to practice," he said. "They knew what to expect from Coach Hall as far as the style of play that he wanted. They knew the offense in and out. We as young players had to follow their lead, because they were so experienced, and they led us in everything they did from practice and the way they carried themselves off the floor, in the dorm, and around the community. Everything they did was very professional and very serious and very intense. They were a great example for all of us."

After the 1977 spring semester, Givens, Robey, Phillips, and Lee organized a summer workout program for the team that included some weight lifting but mainly consisted of pick-up basketball games on weeknights in Alumni Gym—after players had finished their workday on summer jobs or summer classes at UK. "That was a hot gym; there was no air conditioning in there!" Claytor recalled. Sometimes the team played outside on the campus "blue courts." "There were no coaches involved; it was all player-driven," Givens said. "We just divided up teams and said, 'Let's go.' We'd play for two, sometimes three hours." This gave the team a leg up on developing chemistry before official coach-led practices began in mid-October. "It helped immensely, playing with the intensity that we did over the summer," he said. "It kind of set the tone for how we worked all season long."

Macy said the summer conditioning program "was big for me, because I probably came here weighing 155 or 160 pounds soaking wet and had never touched a weight in my life. By transitioning to starting to lift weights, I was able to put on some bulk and strength." The summer heat made Alumni Gym feel "hotter than fire" during pick-up games, he said. "It was good competition because we were playing against each other. Playing each other built mutual respect."

Scott Courts, who arrived on campus that summer from Arvada, Colorado, as a freshman center, recalls hanging out one late afternoon with some of his new teammates in the high-jump pit of the former Shively track, which featured a rubberized running surface. "Rick Robey said, 'Hey, man. I'll give you five bucks if you can run a mile in . . .'—I forget what the time was," he said. "I did that, but there was such closeness among us early on." Courts described Robey and the other seniors "as big brothers" to him and the other underclassmen. "They were great people and natural leaders, almost iconic in their own way of leading," he said. "Mike Phillips was an alternative guy—a rock star. Jack Givens should be the governor, a wonderful conventional leader. And there was Rick Robey, the big hero, the businessman. James Lee was the hammer, the enforcer, the Clint Eastwood. For me, it was like winning the lottery because I was a really tall kid trying to find a suitable sport. I had just given up little league football, and I got a call one night while watching the television series *Hawaii Five-O*. The guy on the other end of the line was a local coach, John Lindenmeyer. He asked, 'Do you play basketball?'

"I said, 'No.'

"'Well, do you want to?'

"I remember putting the phone down and asking my dad (I can still hear the Ventures' *Hawaii Five-O* theme song in the background). I was just a kid. 'Sure. Why not?' That was the beginning of it all for me."

Mike Murphy, who began his second year as a student manager that season, said there was no question in anyone's mind that Givens, Robey, Phillips, and Lee would serve as the core leaders for the 1977–1978 campaign. "Everybody followed them," he said. "If somebody got out of line, they kind of self-policed it. Without a doubt, Jack, Rick, Mike, and James were not going to settle for less than what was actually achieved. I think Joe B. [Hall] knew that, and I think he relied on those guys to deliver the message that he wanted delivered."

Joe Dean Jr. characterized Robey as "a big stud and kind of the enforcer on the team. And we had James Lee, who was kind of the super-sub off the bench who came in and wreaked havoc by driving to the goal and dunking on people. Jack Givens was the leading scorer. He was smart. He was steady, kind of a quiet leader. You always could count on him for a big shot. Kyle Macy was the missing piece they didn't have those three previous years. He was such a great floor leader, great shooter, 89 percent foul shooter, and he kept everybody in line on the floor."

In the book *A Year at the Top*,[4] Lawrenceburg, Kentucky, native William "Bill" Keightley, who served as the basketball program's equipment manager for forty-eight years, described Phillips as "a fierce competitor" who played with a lot of pain during his career. "He has had numerous injuries," he told the book's coauthors, John McGill and Walt Johnson. "Mike always got to practice just before it started, not allowing much time for just sitting around." In a newspaper interview near the end of the season, Phillips described himself as an "independent person. Basketball helps you be a self-sustaining individual. It's not that I have trouble at home. My parents are beautiful people. But I'm independent, I can be myself."[5]

Center Mike Phillips (55) puts up a shot against Mississippi State during his sophomore season on March 8, 1976, as teammate Larry Johnson (12) looks on. Phillips and Rick Robey, both listed as six feet ten inches, were known as Kentucky's original "Twin Towers." (Courtesy of UK Athletics.)

In an audio interview from June 6, 2006,[6] Keightley recalled that Givens was nicknamed Silky "because his movement was so smooth. He just flowed down the floor and had a great left-handed shot." Lee, he continued, "blew out more basketball shoes than any player that's ever been here, and I always accused him of stopping too quick," while Robey was "an elder statesman from the time he arrived. Rick always had an answer and was a joy to work with." If the players wanted something done, "they went to Robey," Ralph Hacker added. "They'd say, 'Rick, we need this done,' and Robey would say, 'Let me see what I can do.'"

Lee remembered no shortage of egos when he arrived on campus as a freshman in 1974. Robey and Phillips played on teams that won state high school basketball championships in Louisiana and Ohio, respectively, while Givens and Lee both played on high school teams that advanced to the Kentucky state high school basketball tournament (Givens twice and Lee once). "We were used to winning and putting all these egos together and taking the ball away from each guy to share in a team," Lee said. "That's special. It takes that to win championships."

Coach Hamilton said that the temperament and inner drive of Givens, Robey, Phillips, and Lee set a foundation for success. "They had tremendous character and had Kentucky in their hearts," he said. "They had a workman's attitude. That was a bunch of guys who were committed; they were focused; they were able to just absorb the moment and not get rattled because it meant so much to them as individuals. To me, that's what stood out more than anything else."

These four seniors may have been gifted with innate leadership skills, but they'd been mentored by their predecessors, too. For example, Givens said that during his freshman year, he learned just about everything he knew about basketball from Kevin Grevey, a standout senior forward on the 1974–1975 Wildcats team that also featured Mike Flynn, Jimmy Dan Conner, and Bob Guyette. "For

Mentors to the Kentucky freshmen in 1974 were, from left, seniors Jimmy Dan Conner, Kevin Grevey, Bob Guyette, Jerry Hale, G. J. Smith, and Mike Flynn. (Courtesy of the University of Kentucky Archives.)

a guy coming into a situation, trying to learn, there was not a better group of guys to learn from than those guys, but Kevin taught me as a freshman how to deal with Coach Hall," Givens recalled. "He said, 'Goose, one of these days you're going to be in the same situation I'm in, where everything that comes out of Coach Hall's mouth is going to be directed toward you, because you're going to be the superstar. You're going to be the man.' I couldn't understand why Coach Hall would get on the best player on the team, because in my mind Grevey was always playing great. I had to practice against him every day, so I was getting the worst of it and seeing the best of it at the same time. Kevin said, 'The thing you have to understand is that you can't pay a lot of attention to what Coach Hall says when he's getting on you. He's saying it to you, but it's meant for the entire team.' When Rick and I were seniors, most of his harshness and criticism was focused on me and Rick. I learned not to let that get me down but to use that to motivate myself."

Lee said that his key mentors from prior Wildcat squads included Grevey, Conner, and his former college roommate Merion Haskins, a native of Campbellsville, Kentucky, who was the second African American Coach Hall recruited when he assumed head coaching duties, behind Reggie Warford, a native of Drakesboro, Kentucky. Haskins "was a key influence in instructing me to prepare for college life," Lee recalled. "It was important to balance college life with the expectations of Kentucky basketball."

The senior leadership of Grevey, Conner, Flynn, and Guyette played a role in Robey's decision to sign with UK as a freshman for the 1974–1975 campaign. "When that group came in as freshmen, they were a highly touted bunch of guys," Robey said. "I think that's one of the big reasons I selected Kentucky over Notre Dame, because of the senior group and the fact that Kentucky already had commitments from Mike Phillips, Danny Hall,[7] Jack Givens, and James Lee. I thought that was going to be a great nucleus of freshmen. Putting the senior group and the freshmen group together I felt like could be a great season for us. And it did turn out to be that type of a season."

Guyette, a fellow center, served as a mentor to Robey on and off the court. "Not only was he a very good basketball player, but he was a good student in the classroom, too," Robey said of Guyette. "That's one thing you have to learn when you get to college. Not only are you there to play basketball, you're also there to get an education. I think Guyette kind of rubbed off on us when it came to that."

For Macy, having to sit out the prior season due to transfer rules "made me appreciate playing, because I'd been playing ever since I could crawl," he said. "That was tough, sitting the whole year, not being able to play competitive games. I love competition. To me,

A capacity crowd watches a 1977 Wildcats game in Rupp Arena. "Big Bertha," the speaker cluster that hung forty-three feet above the center of the arena, was retired after the 2015–2016 season. (Courtesy of the University of Kentucky Archives.)

my game was practice every day, so I was trying to do everything I could in practice, from learning a new system and the discipline of Coach Hall, to learning to get to know the players: what they like to do on the court and their personalities off the court, taking it all in. Getting to play against Larry Johnson every day in practice made me a better player. He was super fast, really strong, and challenged me a lot."

Macy also used his redshirt year to scout the fan base known as Big Blue Nation. Sometimes before home games he'd wander the corridors of the Rupp Arena concourse "because nobody knew me," he said. "I'm not six-eleven, so I could kind of blend into the crowd. I also drove on my own to a couple of conference games to get a feel for the atmosphere and what people were saying. That kind of made me understand the importance of Kentucky basketball."

Chris Gettelfinger, a freshman guard from Knoxville, Tennessee, who earned a spot as a walk-on that year, said that the impact of senior leadership from Givens, Robey, Phillips, and Lee can't be underestimated, from the pick-up games they orchestrated in the summer to the camaraderie they fostered on and off the hardwood. "The only reason we won is because there were seniors," he said. "When you took them out [of a game] for four or five minutes and you put them back in, those guys overcame the biggest odds in the world. Mentally, that's why they were great. They were afraid also, because they wanted to win it [all]. It was their last chance, but they overcame it. The '78 team won the championship on mentally being more prepared, being older, and overcoming."

That's not to say the underclassmen didn't want to win a national championship, but it was the last go-around for the seniors. "Maybe when you have a little sense of desperation you just don't ever let up," Tim Stephens said. "That was pretty much the attitude of everybody. It was a situation where we were of one mind and one accord."

2

Grueling Practices

One sticky September afternoon in Central Kentucky, six-foot, ten-inch freshman center Scott Courts was hunched over on his hands and knees on the Shively track, drenched in sweat and gasping for air. He'd just run several 220-yard dashes as part of the team's preconditioning program and felt as if he were going to vomit. Then a pair of tennis shoes entered his field of vision, and when he looked up, he saw Coach Parsons hovering in front of him, with a whistle around his neck and holding a clipboard.

"Young man," he barked to Courts, "I don't want you to worry. If something happens to you now, if you die, we're going to bury your heart, balls, and your hooves, just like you would a good thoroughbred."

Coach Parsons was kidding, of course, but he always pushed the players to give their all. That year's preconditioning program, which coincided with the start of the academic semester and continued until mid-October when formal practices began as per NCAA rules, consisted of weight training and light running on Mondays, Wednesdays, and Fridays and longer runs on Tuesdays and Thursdays. "We'd break huddle in our running program every day," Macy

The 1977–1978 Wildcats outscored their opponents by 459 points during the season. Seated from left to right are Coach Joe B. Hall, Jay Shidler, Dwane Casey, Kyle Macy, Jack Givens, Tim Stephens, Chris Gettelfinger, Truman Claytor, and Assistant Coach Dick Parsons. Standing from left to right are Assistant Trainer Walt McCombs, Head Student Manager Don Sullivan, LaVon Williams, Scott Courts, Mike Phillips, Rick Robey, Chuck Aleksinas, Fred Cowan, James Lee, Assistant Coach Leonard Hamilton, and Assistant Coach Joe Dean Jr. (Courtesy of the University of Kentucky Archives.)

said. "As we'd break, we'd say, 'Number one,' because that was the goal, to finish number one." Over the course of that month and a half the team built up to twelve timed 220-yard dashes in 32 seconds, with a one-minute interval between each one, and as much weight lifting as they could muster. "We didn't try to be physical; we just were," said Coach Parsons, who played guard at UK for three seasons under Adolph Rupp, beginning with the 1958–1959 campaign. "We credit a lot of that to good conditioning and weight training. Back in that time not every team would do that."

Weight lifting was a new focus that year, and things got competitive. Mike Murphy remembered an area of the weight-room wall at Shively that listed the top UK athletes who lifted the most pounds. The names of UK football greats Jerry Blanton, Art Still, and Derrick Ramsey often appeared there, he said, but before long the names of basketball players like James Lee, Dwane Casey, Rick Robey, and Mike Phillips earned spots in the top five. "They were reaching those marks," Murphy said.

Pat Etcheberry, UK's strength and conditioning coach at the time, recalled that some of the football players told him, "'Hey, those basketball guys are supposed to be wimpy,' and all of a sudden they were lifting just as much as they were. We did a lot of core exercises and a lot of shoulder exercises, because in basketball for shooting and rebounding you have to have strong shoulders—not a huge chest, but very strong in the shoulders, legs, and core." When Macy arrived on campus after transferring from Purdue, he appeared leery of weight lifting at first, Etcheberry said, but he quickly came around. "It was a matter of selling him. I had to tell him, 'When you lift, it's going to make you a better player. You're going to shoot better. You're going to rebound better. You're going to have better stamina on the court. You won't get hurt as much as other players.'" (Later in his UK career, Macy modeled for several photos used to illustrate weight lifting and stretching exercises described in a book penned by Coach Hall and Dwane Casey titled *Kentucky's Conditioning Program for Basketball*.)

One exercise, known as a step-up, involved a player's stepping firmly with one foot onto a twenty-four-inch-high bench with a weight bar balanced on his shoulders. He would then drive his body weight forward as he brought the other foot onto the bench. Many of the basketball players achieved the benchmark of 225 pounds for this exercise, Etcheberry recalled, but James Lee was able to step onto the raised bench while balancing 275 pounds on his shoulders. "He was a monster with that exercise," he said.

The Wildcats continued to lift weights year-round as part of their conditioning program. "It helped us reduce the number of injuries, and the players performed better and shot better through the year, because the goal was to keep them ready for the NCAA Tournament," said Etcheberry, who was also UK's track coach that year. "We were lifting all through the season, not to show everybody how tough we were, just to make sure we won. The whole thing was based on how many 'Ws' you got, and winning the last game of the season." He challenged the players during workouts just as the other coaches did, and if anyone slacked off, Coach Hall would hear about it. "My job was to make their lives as miserable as possible," Etcheberry said. "I told the players, 'You have to concentrate as much in the weight room as you do on the court, because if you do something wrong with bad technique, you could injure yourself. I want to prevent injuries in the weight room, not cause them.'"

Student manager Tony Sosby said that the weight-lifting sessions were "a competition to be the strongest, to be the fittest. During that season it was not a problem to get them to go to weight lifting. They thrived to do it."

Sophomore guard Tim Stephens, who was rehabilitating a torn anterior cruciate ligament from the previous season, described the preconditioning program as a bonding experience for the team. "You always felt pressure to produce, but Coach Parsons had a good practical outlook on things," he added. "I've always felt that his contribution as a coach may have been overlooked through the years. I was able to do the running pretty well. But when I had to bear a lot of weight on my knee, that was so hard for me, because I could only bend it to a certain point, and then it wouldn't bear any more weight. I had to compensate by using my other leg twice as much as I probably should have."

Once mid-October rolled around, official practices began. Coach Hall printed a schedule for each one. Bill Keightley and the managers made sure that the players had everything they needed in the locker room before practice, including shoes and workout gear. "During practice we ran a lot of the drills," Mike Murphy recalled.

The 1977–1978 Wildcats were deep at the guard spot, including juniors Truman Claytor (22) and Dwane Casey (20). (Courtesy of the University of Kentucky Archives.)

"Oftentimes we would participate in practice itself—running scout team stuff and things like that. We played pick-up games before and after practice with the guys."

Tripp Ramsey, the team's graduate assistant coach who had played junior varsity basketball at UK, arrived at practices dressed for competition, since this Wildcat squad had an odd number of players. "We had three plays: six, eight, and ten, and there was some additional guard offense," said Ramsey, who is the son of former UK guard Frank Ramsey, a star guard from UK's 1951 NCAA National Championship team. "A lot of times, just out of the blue, we would run some of Coach Rupp's offense. To run a guard offense, you always needed an even number of players. I was the odd player that had to run guard offense for the whole year. I enjoyed it."

Sosby, who served as a student manager during five UK basketball seasons, said that the intensity of practices set the 1977–1978 team apart from others. "That senior class didn't like being shown up in practice, especially if it was one of the younger guys," he recalled. "That particular year we had from seven to ten fights during practice; I'm talking connected fist on face. They'd eventually break it up, and Joe B. [Hall] would say, 'Get yer butts in the shower,' or something like that. As a young person, I remember thinking, 'Ok. These two people just got through fighting. And you're going to send them to the showers together?!'" But the tussles were soon forgotten, he said, and the next day whichever teammates had been fighting "looked like two friends. Even in the years following, we didn't have nearly as many fights. Not that that determines competition or something about a team, but I think it built a lot of team, a lot of family. They would fight for each other in games. I saw that in practice."

On the first day of practice, Fred Cowan inadvertently cut James Lee above the eye with the corner of his elbow after pulling down a rebound. "He had to have some stitches, and it just put fear in my heart," Cowan said. "Lee was a big man, and I was a freshman. I told him I didn't mean to do it. He was OK with it. If he wasn't, I would have known about it quickly. Practice was something else. You would know if somebody was mad at you."

Freshman center Chuck Aleksinas shared a similar memory from his clashes with fellow center Mike Phillips. Three or four times during practices, he said, "I hit him with an inadvertent elbow, and he'd have stitches. Mike never got angry. He was just a nice guy, no matter what. Looking back on it, if I was a senior and somebody was coming in and trying to shove me and push me and this and that, I'd probably get a little aggravated. But he was always even-keeled. He treated the younger guys like you weren't a freshman. Mike would offer me rides to practices and functions. Seniors as a rule don't really associate with freshmen like that."

The second day of practice altered the season's trajectory for sophomore guard Jay Shidler. The players were walking off the court after what they thought was a full day of workouts when Coach Hall called them back for one more drill. "We ran what was called an eleven-man drill, up and down the court individually getting passes from guys at certain spots on the court, running the length of the court, laying it in, and doing the same thing coming back," said Shidler, who had started in all games the previous season. "But you had to go as fast as you could." During his second time down the court, he rose for a layup and felt a sharp pain in his right foot when he landed. He didn't think much of it at the time, but the pain persisted the next day, so he had it X-rayed. The first one showed no anomalies, but the third X-ray revealed a small hairline fracture in the fifth metatarsal of his right foot. "I could have played, I guess, but it was so early in the year they decided to put a pin in there, a screw. I was in a cast for six weeks or so," he said. It marked the first serious injury of his young athletic career and set him back about ten weeks. "It was hard to take, but I tried to stay in condition by

Jay "The Blond Bomber" Shidler (right) poses with Coach Hall in 1977. In 1976 Shidler was named "Mr. Basketball" for Illinois as a high school senior. (Courtesy of the University of Kentucky Archives.)

doing pushups and sit-ups," he said. "I was at practice every day in spirit. I wish I could have contributed more, but that's just the way it worked out."

Chris Gettelfinger recalled one practice that was attended by several high school coaches who were on campus for a clinic run by Coach Hall. Gettelfinger sustained a deep gash above his eye that sent him to the training room for an evaluation by athletic trainer Walt McCombs. Within a few minutes, Coach Hall appeared in the room and asked if McCombs could suture the wound so Gettelfinger could return to the floor. The laceration required seven stitches. Coach Hall said, "'Chris, if you feel like it, I want you to come back out there as soon as you can with your stitches, and I want you to finish practice,'" Gettelfinger recalled. "As soon as Walt stitched me up, I came out, and Joe B. said in front of the coaches, 'Look, he's coming back out here. We're a tough-minded team.' He used that; he preached being physical. I knew I had to do that. I'm proud that I came back out there; there wasn't even a question. I would have come back out there even with just Steri-Strips."

During another practice, LaVon Williams suffered a blow to the inside of his top lip, which sent blood gushing. "All they'd do was stitch you up and put you right back out there," Williams said. "There was no workman's comp; it was all blood and guts. If you boxed a guy out the wrong way, he'd bust your lip if you didn't keep your hands up. It was a tough grind."

George L. Fletcher recalled one practice in which Coach Parsons leapt on a bunch of players who had fallen on the floor while scrambling for a loose ball. "He knew he needed to inject some levity in the situation before somebody got up and started swinging," Fletcher said. "He just dove on the pile."

Things could get contentious during "take the charge," a drill in which a player has to take a charge from another player driving toward the basket. The player who takes the charge then has to

Behind the scenes, several UK students assisted the 1977–1978 Wildcats. Pictured from left to right in the front row are manager Mike Murphy, statistician Barbara Higgins, manager Tony Sosby, and statistician Bill Leitsch. Pictured in the back row from left to right are head student manager Don Sullivan, manager George L. Fletcher, trainer Mark Farrell, manager John Kinney, and manager Rob Bolton. (Courtesy of George L. Fletcher.)

quickly pick himself up from the floor under the basket and dive on a basketball that a manager rolls toward the free-throw line. Next, the player picks himself up and dribbles toward the right side of the basket, where two managers await with handheld, padded football blocking dummies to contest his shot. "If the managers didn't hit the guys hard enough, Coach Hall would bring somebody else in to hit them," Fletcher recalled. "He was trying to toughen them up. Sometimes it would get heated, but sometimes we'd knock somebody down, and everybody would just roll over laughing because it got to be so crazy, tackling these guys."

Practices were so grueling that it wasn't uncommon for a player to burn through a pair of high-top basketball shoes in one day. "What I noticed in the very first practice was the smell of the rubber burning," Murphy said. "[Rick] Robey could burn through a pair of shoes in one practice. That's how much pressure he could put on a pair of shoes."

Givens remembers Coach Hall's halting some practices "because we were going at it so hard that he was afraid people would get hurt. A lot of coaches would love to get that kind of intensity from their players. If we ever did get sent home, it was because we were working too hard, and Coach Hall just felt like we didn't need to work anymore. We were getting everything done that needed to be done. Rick and myself as captains led that charge. All of the other players jumped onboard and said, 'Hey. Let's go.'"

Even the seasoned seniors could lose their cool. Lee said that he and Robey sparred a few times. "Rick had this knack for sticking his rear end out on picks," he said. "I stopped practice one day to get that straightened out. I said, 'I'm on this team. I know the pick is there, but you don't have to engage in physical activity.' Little things like that happened all the time. Defensively, Coach [Hall] wanted us to be aggressive. Sometimes we'd get a little physical, but the next day we'd be laughing about it. That's why we enjoyed the games. Our games were easy, but the practices were brutal."

Scrutiny from coaches during practice accompanied the demanding physical play. For example, if you stepped to the right when you were supposed to step to the left and Coach Hall had his back turned, "he knew what you did," Chuck Aleksinas said. "I think we all felt that no matter what, if you made a mistake, it was going to be seen. There was an unbelievable focus of trying not to do things wrong. Sometimes it was a little bit too much. A lot of the players say we didn't have fun. It was really more of a job that year. That's not a bad thing; it's just the way it was. It made for very seri-

Assistant Coach Leonard Hamilton pictured in 1974, the same year he joined Coach Hall's staff. Hamilton is currently the head coach of men's basketball at Florida State University. (Courtesy of the University of Kentucky Archives.)

ous practices. We had a job to do, and we did it. You can't criticize anybody on how they got to a championship when they win it."

According to Tim Stephens, of the many preseason scrimmages between the starting five players and those who weren't, the second-stringers beat the starting five once, while another matchup ended in a tie. "That gives you an idea of the intensity of our practices," he said.

Tough as the sessions were, Coach Parsons didn't recall a bad practice from that season. "That's kind of unusual," he said. "It was a team that just didn't have any issues. They were cordial with each other. You didn't see any two people that stayed off to themselves. It was a pleasant year because you had good kids, good focus, playing well. The thing is, everyone thought we were going to win it all. That's what made it difficult."

An only child, Rob Bolton routinely called his mom and dad to share his enthusiasm about his behind-the-scenes experience as a student manager and his observations about the team chemistry unfolding before him. "I can remember going back to the dorm at night to call them and say, 'Guess what I got to do today? I got to referee a scrimmage. I'm telling you I got to referee the number one and the number two teams in the country,' because the second five were good. I would say, 'That's a pretty high level of basketball that I'm out there trying to officiate.'"

3

Farewell to Rupp

The Wildcats were ranked number two in the Associated Press preseason poll behind North Carolina and their star point guard, Phil Ford Jr., the team that had lost to Marquette in the NCAA Championship game the prior season. As smooth as practices were going, the pressure of the upcoming season was palpable and could get under the skin of players and coaches if they thought about it too much. In fact, Truman Claytor remembered Coach Hall telling the players once before a practice that his own job was on the line if the Wildcats didn't bring home the NCAA national trophy in March 1978.

One day in Memorial Coliseum, Coach Hall didn't like the effort he was seeing from the players in practice, so he instructed each of them to run ten walls. The "wall" was a drill in which each player would stand at the bottom of an aisle in Memorial Coliseum and, when instructed, run up each step, touch each step with his hands on the way up, touch the wall at the top of the coliseum steps, turn around, and repeat the same motions on the way down. Coach Hall noticed that James Lee didn't reach the coliseum floor on the way down before turning around to run back up, and he called him on it.

"How many walls does James have?" he remembered asking a manager.

"Six."

"I said, 'No, he hasn't. He hasn't got any,' and James was right there.

"James said, 'What do you mean?'

"I said, 'You haven't come to the floor, so you still got ten to run.' He walked off, left."

Lee, the coveted sixth man off the bench and a key team leader, exited the coliseum, got into his car, and drove to his home in Lexington. When he arrived, his father's car was blocking the driveway, so James parked on the street. He remembered thinking it was odd for his father, Rev. Albert B. Lee, who pastored Greater Liberty Baptist Church in Lexington, to be home in the midafternoon of a workweek. "He was never home at this time," Lee said. Unbeknownst to him, someone had notified Reverend Lee about what had transpired at practice that day.

"I walked up to the porch, and my dad was sitting there," Lee recalled. "I reached for the doorknob to go into the house, and he said, 'You can't go in there.'

"I said, 'Excuse me?'

"He said, 'Aren't you supposed to have practice today?'

"I said, 'Well, I had a little incident there.'

"He said, 'Well, why don't you tell me about it?'

"I said, 'We had a little disagreement, and I felt like I was fed up.'

"He said, 'You made a commitment. You haven't fulfilled your commitment. Until you fulfill your commitment, you cannot walk in this house.' Those were my options. So that evening I went back over and apologized to the coaches and the team and was accepted back."

It remains a mystery who called Reverend Lee to let him know

The Soviet National Team's Vladimir Tkachenko (left) and UK's James Lee exchange gifts at midcourt in Memorial Coliseum prior to tip-off. (Courtesy of the *Lexington Herald-Leader*. Photo by E. Martin Jessee.)

his son had walked away from practice that day. "I never asked him about it, and he never brought it up," said James Lee, who was the steel half of "Silk and Steel," along with fellow Lexingtonian Givens. "One regret I have is that I never asked my father who called. It's one of those mysteries of life." Kyle Macy looked back on that incident as one that could have altered the season's outcome. "If you think about it, if he did quit, how would that have changed our team?" he asked. "Things just kind of have to fall into place."

As crisp fall temperatures began to blanket the Commonwealth, the team traveled to Hazard, Maysville, and Northern Kentucky University for preseason intrasquad Blue-White scrimmages,[1] where fans packed gyms to watch their beloved Wildcats. For Rob Bolton, who was raised in Louisville as a diehard UK supporter, the game at the Hazard High School gym led to a unique encounter with a fan. "All my heroes growing up were primarily Kentucky basketball players," Bolton said. "If Kevin Grevey wore a certain shoe, you could bet I was out hunting that shoe. I was the stereotypical kid for all of that. I had no choice. My parents were that way; my grandparents were that way."

The team was still in the gym locker room, and Bolton was standing underneath one of the backboards with a basketball under each arm, anticipating warm-ups. He heard an elderly woman near courtside yell, "Sonny! Sonny!" to get his attention, and he turned to approach her.

"She asked, 'Are those the basketballs that the boys are gonna use?'"

"I said, 'Yes, ma'am.'"

"'May I see one?'"

"I said, 'Sure,' and handed her one from under my arm. She took it and caressed it like you would a child or a pet. The ball had 'Kentucky' stamped on it, and she said, 'Do they all say this?'"

"I said, 'Yes, ma'am.'"

"She said, 'I want to thank you. When they come out I will have got to see them in person, and I can really die happily knowing that I got to see my team.'

"I'm like, 'Are you kidding me?'"

That exchange, he said, transported Bolton back to memories of his grandparents, listening to longtime broadcaster Cawood Ledford call UK games on the radio. They had floor-register heat, he said, and his grandmother would "stand over that heat, and my grandfather would look over at her and say, 'I don't think they're going to win tonight.' They were so wrapped up in Kentucky basketball. That's where I come from, so it was an interesting moment to see a lady get so taken by getting a chance to touch the ball that [the team] is going to touch. It was a grounding thing. You realize how unifying Kentucky basketball is to a poor, disrespected state. It's the sport of the people."

The importance of Kentucky basketball to the citizens of the Commonwealth wasn't lost on the players, either, including those who grew up elsewhere. "I realize that everybody in the state of Kentucky is not well off," Knoxville native Chris Gettelfinger said. "Some people are sick, others are poor. There were coal strikes when we were playing. A lot of people's lives aren't perfect, but Kentucky basketball is the single thing in the state of Kentucky that makes people's lives better. When we'd scrimmage in these small towns, my gosh, the whole town would turn out! And when we were going to play Notre Dame that year, we went to Louisville's Freedom Hall for a practice, and it was packed. There were fifteen thousand people there."

Prior to the final intrasquad scrimmage at Northern Kentucky University, the Wildcats hosted the Russian national team in a matchup played in Memorial Coliseum on November 11, 1977, and beat them 109–75. "That was a team that had huge success at the national level," Macy said. "They were big in size, shot it well, and

Truman Claytor (right) in action against Southern Methodist University, Kentucky's first opponent of regular season play. (Courtesy of the University of Kentucky Archives.)

experienced. We handled them pretty easily. That may have been the first indication that our team could be special. It wasn't even a close game." Shidler recalled that at one point in the game James Lee threw down one of his thunderous one-handed dunks over the seven-foot, three-inch Russian center Vladimir Tkachenko "like he wasn't there. The place went crazy." After the contest the Soviet Union coach Alexandr Gomelsky described the Wildcats as a "beautiful team. Best team in U.S. Best team I ever look. Not in Olympic Games, not in University Games do I see better."[2]

UK's first game of the regular season was played in Rupp Arena against Southern Methodist University (SMU) on November 26, 1977. The Wildcats won handily 110–86, but Macy found himself shaking off some rust early in the game. "The first time I ran out on the court at Rupp, the hair on my neck stood up; I was so nervous," he recalled. After tip-off, SMU jumped into a zone. The Wildcats had practiced a zone offense, but Macy couldn't remember what it was called. "Fortunately, Jack or somebody got fouled, so I ran over to the bench," he said. "Coach Hall was already chewing on somebody else, so I went down to Coach Parsons and asked, 'Coach, what's the name of that zone offense?' He told me what it was. Then Coach Hall saw me talking to Coach Parsons. At halftime going into the locker room, he jumped on me and said, 'I'm the head coach here. The sooner you learn that, the better off you'll be. If you don't understand that you better just transfer out of here.'" Givens and Robey led the Wildcats with 30 and 23 points, respectively.

During home and away games Coach Hall brandished a rolled-up game program in one hand while he carried out his duties. He formed the habit during his tenure as an assistant for Coach Adolph Rupp, who used the program to mark Kentucky's starting lineup. "Then I would take it in my hand and go to the scorer's table and report the starters," Coach Hall said. "Occasionally, I'd keep that program in my hand. When I became head coach, I developed a habit of having that program." Rolling up a program properly before the tip-off of each game required attention to certain details. "If it was too thick, we had to take out pages," head student manager Don Sullivan said. "It had to be rolled up so it was durable but not in his way." According to LaVon Williams, Coach Hall also used the program to get the attention of players by "hitting you outside your leg, outside your head, or on your butt with that program if you had done something wrong." Or if a referee's call didn't go Kentucky's way. Shidler likely endured more inadvertent whacks from rolled-up programs than any other player that season because Coach Hall "would always make me sit next to him on the bench," he said. "I still have welts on my lower left leg from where he would beat me with the program (laughs). As a matter of fact, when I heard they were putting a statue of him out in front of the new Wildcat Coal Lodge[3] and he's got a program in his hand, I was like, 'Where's my statue sitting there and him beating me with it?'"

Also before every game, Sullivan and his fellow student managers used training tape to mark an "X" on the seat of Hall's chair on the bench "so he could look for that chair and make sure he was sitting in the right one." (One of Robey's pregame rituals was to tuck away a medal of Saint Christopher[4]—a gift from his mother—between his athletic socks. He also made sure to practice left- and right-handed hook shots and free throws during warm-ups.)

The next game was against Indiana in Rupp Arena on December 5, a contest that was tied eleven times before Kentucky ended the first half with a 33–28 advantage.[5] Even though Indiana star Mike Woodson fouled out with a little over twelve minutes left in the second half, his fellow Hoosiers cut UK's lead to 7 points with a little over three minutes remaining. The Wildcats then pulled away and won 78–64, led again by Givens and Robey, who scored 22 and 20 points, respectively.

For the season's first game away from home, the team traveled to Lawrence, Kansas, for a contest with the Kansas Jayhawks at Allen Fieldhouse on December 10. Weighing on the mind of Coach Hall was the health of his predecessor and former boss, who was hospitalized at UK Medical Center in Lexington, gravely ill with cancer.

Scott Courts (44) anticipates a rebound against Portland State University in Rupp Arena on December 16, 1977. (Courtesy of the University of Kentucky Archives.)

"I remember the [game] preparation and knowing that Coach Rupp was in the hospital when we left Lexington," Hall said. "Everyone was uneasy about his status and hoping that he would recover in some way. It was always on my mind, and I think I carried a lot of that over to the players."

The timing of the Wildcats-Jayhawks matchup was ironic. After all, Coach Rupp, a native of Halstead, Kansas, had been a reserve for the Jayhawks from 1919 to 1923 under Coach Forrest "Phog" Allen. He had also been tutored there by Dr. James Naismith, the man who invented the game of basketball itself. To Coach Hall, any trip to Lawrence was nostalgic "because when I was Coach's assistant and we played Kansas, he and I often went to visit Phog Allen in his home. To see Coach Rupp and his respect for Coach Allen was a great experience. To sit in a room with those two is a memory that I'll never forget."

The Wildcats turned the ball over 22 times and had 17 fewer shots from the field compared with the Jayhawks, but hung on to win 73–66 on clutch free-throw shooting.[6] The game marked Shidler's first return to action since his foot injury. "I made a couple of baskets, and I got a steal late in the game that kind of sealed the deal," Shidler said. "I felt good about it." Macy and Phillips led the Wildcats with 15 and 14 points, respectively, and the team pulled down a total of 44 rebounds, only one better than the 43 collected by the Jayhawks. On the return flight to Lexington, word came to the pilots that Coach Rupp had died soon after the game had ended. He was seventy-six. "We announced that to our players, and we had a prayer," Coach Hall said. "We all had a sad feeling for Coach Rupp and hope that he got word of our victory before he passed." Casey described the timing of Coach Rupp's passing as paradoxical. "You think about the irony of him playing at Kansas, he was from Kansas, and we were playing Kansas, his alma mater, and he passed away," Casey said. "It gives you goosebumps to think about that."

While Rupp's death was not unexpected, it marked the end of an era for a man who built a tradition of excellence at UK that has stood the test of time. Over a period of forty-two years, he led teams to four NCAA national titles and finished his career in 1972 with a win-loss record of 876–190 (82 percent). He was inducted into the Naismith Memorial Basketball Hall of Fame in 1969. "When he was gone, it did make an impact on me, because a big part of something that's bigger than life itself was gone," recalled sophomore guard Tim Stephens, who grew up in Revelo, Kentucky. "I had laid in my bed and listened to games he had coached since I was big enough to turn on a little transistor radio."

One day before the team left Lexington for the trip to Lawrence, Coach Parsons and UK's longtime team physician, Dr. V. A. Jackson, paid a visit to Coach Rupp.

"Dr. Jackson said, 'Coach, is there anything we can do for you?'" Parsons recalled. "We knew he wasn't in very good shape. Coach Rupp said, 'There's not really anything you can do for me, but if I don't whip this thing, I'll tell you what you can do. By God, you just go have a drink with your friends.'

"Dr. Jackson said, 'Do you want us to have that drink on the way to the cemetery or on the way back?'

"He said, 'On the way out to the cemetery. I won't be with you on the way back.' That's the last time I saw Coach Rupp."

Two days after Rupp's death, Joe Kemp, editorial editor for UK's student newspaper *The Kentucky Kernel,* reflected on Rupp's influence. "Through his success in basketball and his ability to communicate effectively, Rupp gave this institution a national name, put it on the map," Kemp wrote.[7] "Some scholars might dismiss such an observation as nonsense, that a basketball coach couldn't be that important. But Adolph Rupp and UK were synonymous. And his influence transcended the campus. He may have been Kentucky's most powerful figure in the 1950s." Kemp went on to note that Rupp taught a basketball class at UK and rewarded each of his students with an A. "His reasoning was simply that no one could learn

Kentucky center Chuck Aleksinas (right) defends fellow freshman Kevin Vesey of the Iona Gaels. (Courtesy of the *Lexington Herald-Leader.* Photo by Mike Kearney.)

basketball from Adolph Rupp and not get an A. The man was not encumbered by modesty."

In an issue of *The Cats' Pause* that month, editor and publisher Oscar Combs credited Rupp with helping to build college basketball into an American pastime. "Adolph Rupp is the man responsible, more than anyone else, for the game's great popularity," Combs wrote.[8] "He owns so many records that it is easy to overlook most of them. He won more games than any other coach—and that is the one record envied by all coaches."

Robey didn't know Coach Rupp well but said that he helped him land a spot on the USA basketball team that competed in the 1975 Pan American Games. "They weren't allowing freshmen to try out, but Rupp had pull with the Olympic Committee," Robey recalled. Rupp facilitated an invitation for Robey to try out for the team in Salt Lake City, where about 120 players competed for 12 spots. Robey made the cut. "If it wasn't for Rupp's pull on the Olympic Committee, I probably wouldn't have gotten to play on that team," he said. "Heck, that's where I got to know Robert Parish, who I ended up playing with on the [Boston] Celtics. I also played with Otis Birdsong, Ernie Grunfeld, Norm Cook, and Johnny Davis, a lot of the guys I got to know once I got to the NBA, and also I got to play against in the college game."

In the opinion of Ralph Hacker, Coach Rupp's passing had little impact on the 1977–1978 Wildcats. "Coach Rupp was not close to this team," he said. "Of course, they knew him, but Coach Rupp didn't come around to practice a lot. I think he felt unwelcome to come around, for some reason. He didn't feel comfortable. That was always my feeling about it. I had lunch with him about once a week when he was ill."

After the victory in Kansas, the Wildcats played a string of four home games, the first against South Carolina on December 12. Before tip-off, more than twenty-three thousand spectators stood to honor Rupp's passing while a recording of his recitation of Rudyard Kipling's poem "When Earth's Last Picture Is Painted" played over the arena's sound system. Gamecocks coach Frank McGuire was quoted as saying, "You'd have to have all the saints praying for you to beat this team."[9] Kentucky prevailed 84–65, and Robey led the team with 19 points and 11 rebounds, while Givens and Macy added 18 points each.

The next two opponents were part of the annual UK Invitational Tournament[10]: Portland State University on December 16 and St. John's University on December 17. UK beat Portland State handily 114–88, and while Givens led the Wildcats with 26 points, the team enjoyed contributions from several reserves, including 17 points and 7 rebounds from center Chuck Aleksinas and 12 points from Tim Stephens. The following day, Kentucky captured the UK Invitational title by beating nineteenth-ranked St. John's 102–72. Five Wildcats scored in double figures, led by 20 points from Phillips. After the game, St. John's coach Lou Carnesecca described the Wildcats as being "like a big, roaring mountain coming down at you, suffocating you. And I don't mean that to be funny because UK isn't a funny team. They're a great, great team."[11]

Six days later, number-one-ranked UK hosted unranked Iona, which was coached by the late Jim Valvano and featured the six-foot, eleven-inch freshman center Jeff Ruland. The Gaels made things interesting early in the game by building a 21–19 lead. The Wildcats switched from man-to-man defense to a 1-3-1 zone and built a 44–26 halftime lead.[12] In the second half, Kentucky rolled to a 104–65 victory led by seniors Givens, Lee, and Phillips, who finished with 18, 17, and 15 points, respectively. The effort by Givens moved him past Louie Dampier into fifth place on UK's all-time scoring list.[13]

Next, the team traveled to Louisville's Freedom Hall for a New Year's Eve matchup in front of 16,869 fans against the Fighting Irish

Dwane Casey (left) shakes Truman Claytor's hand while the Wildcats wait in a hallway prior to game time. (Courtesy of the University of Kentucky Archives.)

of Notre Dame, whose roster included future NBA stars Kelly Tripucka, Bill Laimbeer, and Orlando Woolridge. The Wildcats had a 42–34 lead going into halftime but fell behind 66–63 in the second half before Kyle Macy scored 8 straight points to put them back on top 71–66 with about thirty seconds left in the game.[14] Kentucky held on to win 73–68, and at the end of the game Macy received the Shively Memorial Plaque for his performance. The award was presented by Notre Dame in memory of the late UK Athletic Director Bernie Shively to the Most Valuable Player in the Kentucky–Notre Dame Game. Macy and Givens each scored 18 points in the contest. "It was tight down the stretch, and I was able to make a drive and make a free throw," Macy recalled. "Helping us win that game made me feel like I kind of fit in. The rust had been shaken off after sitting out the prior year."

Known for his steadiness under pressure, Macy also remains one of best free-throw shooters in the history of Kentucky men's basketball. He and Jodie Meeks are tied as career leaders in free-throw percentage with a minimum of 200 attempts: 89 percent, which the players achieved in 1978–1980 and 2007–2009, respectively. In the book *A Year at the Top,* Macy described his free-throw technique, a ritual emulated by young Wildcat fans across the Commonwealth during his three-year tenure. "I place my toe exactly where I want it on the line and reach down to wipe my hands on my socks to remove any moisture," he told the authors. "Then I receive the ball. My feet are apart at a medium distance, and even on the line, giving me a comfortable, well-balanced feeling. I dribble the ball three times then crouch. The less movement, the less chance of mistake, so my only movement with the ball is upward and forward in a smooth motion. The left hand is at the side of the ball, helping to guide it. I aim at the front part of the hoop. I have a fairly high arch on the shot, as a high arch improves the chances of the ball going through. Before shooting, I exhale. I shoot with my fingers, trying not to have the ball in the palm of my hand. And as I release the ball I give it a little backspin with my fingertips."

Macy's knack for consistency at point guard illustrates a fundamental truth about this team: there were no overall flaws. They had good long-range shooters, could overpower opponents inside, and played solid man-to-man and zone defenses. A sense of balance characterized the coaching staff as well. For example, Macy described the calm demeanor of Coach Parsons as a steadying counter to Coach Hall's tirades during games. "Coach Parsons was good about bringing [Coach Hall] back and getting his focus back in on the game," Macy said. "He had been an outstanding player; he'd been through it. Leonard Hamilton was a real good recruiter but also a good communicator off the floor. Joe Dean had a youthful enthusiasm. They [all] complemented each other."

These Cats were clicking.

4

Christening Wildcat Lodge

During the break between UK's fall and spring semesters, the team moved from their digs in Holmes Hall to Joe B. Hall Wildcat Lodge, a new, freestanding dorm for basketball players that featured private rooms, private bathrooms, beds long enough to accommodate seven-foot-tall body frames, four guest rooms, and a basement with two pinball machines, a pool table, a ping-pong table, a large-screen television set, a large sectional couch, steam room, and a projection meeting room.[1] Coach Hall helped raise money for the $700,000-plus facility, which was paid for by donations from boosters, construction companies, and leaders in the state's coal-mining industry. Inspired in part by Bryant Hall on the campus of the University of Alabama, which opened in 1965 and housed Crimson Tide football and men's basketball teams for more than three decades, the five-level Wildcat Lodge featured a double atrium in the area where the players lived. "I didn't want any architectural feature to separate my players," Hall told *Sunday Herald-Leader* reporter Gail Green in the early summer of 1978.[2] "That can lead to all sorts of interior conflicts and fractionalism. Now the players can talk to each other, no matter which floor they live on. No one needs to feel isolated."

Joe B. Hall Wildcat Lodge as it appeared in later years. It was razed in November 2012 after being replaced earlier that year by the new Wildcat Coal Lodge. (Courtesy of UK Athletics.)

Lexington interior designer Barbara Ricke "went to great lengths to make everything about Wildcat Lodge the utmost in masculinity," Gail Green wrote. "Flatly refusing to decorate in Kentucky blue, she proved the appropriateness of her decision with the final product. The Lodge sports a timeless sense of good taste in natural earthy tones."

Joe Dean Jr. described Wildcat Lodge as "something special, and I think it probably gave the players a sense of appreciation, that Kentucky basketball really was a highly valued team that so many people would put so much into a facility for them to live in. I think it added to the attitude of that team as we were going through that year." As it was being constructed, Dean, Coach Parsons, and the student managers would stop by after some practices to pick up trash and sweep sawdust off the floor. "That was Coach Parsons's big thing: 'Let's go up to the lodge and clean it up so the workers can see what they're doing tomorrow,'" Don Sullivan said. "It wasn't something we didn't want to do; it was kind of exciting. The most unique feature about that place was you had a two-sided fireplace between the living room and dining room by the entrance. The veneer front of it [the fireplace] was made of coal on both sides. It was pretty neat."

After Dwane Casey moved a box of his belongings, a few hangers of clothes, and bedding from Holmes Hall to his new room in Wildcat Lodge, the comfy atmosphere impressed him. "I just remember moving into this big beautiful room with a king-size bed," Casey said. "I'd never slept in a king-size bed before. We all had rocking-chair recliners with a footrest. It was so nice."

The team physician, Dr. V. A. Jackson, and his wife, Marie, a nurse, moved in with the team and assumed a role as houseparents—but not without sacrifice. According to Marie Jackson, one day her husband came home and brought up the idea of serving the basketball program in this capacity.

"I said, 'But we just built a new home that was exactly like I wanted it!'" Jackson recalled.

"He said, 'I know, but I feel like this is something that the Good Lord wants us to do, because we can really be parents to these boys. They're just kids. They're lonely, and we can be parents for them.'

"I laughed at him and said, 'Honey, I've got to pray a long time about this.'

"The next day he asked, 'Have you prayed enough about this?'

"I said, 'What do you think?'

"He said, 'I think that we're supposed to do it.'

"I said, 'Let's put a sign in the front yard for sale by owner. Let's don't call in a realtor. If someone decides that they want to buy our house, then I feel like that's what we should do. We should move in.'"

The late Dr. V. A. Jackson (right) poses with his wife, Marie, and Coach Joe B. Hall on the day the Jacksons agreed to serve as houseparents at Wildcat Lodge. (Courtesy of Marie Jackson.)

The very next day the Jacksons accepted a purchase offer from the owner of the now-defunct Continental Inn in Lexington, and within a matter of weeks they moved into Wildcat Lodge. They took their role as houseparents seriously. "I wanted to instill in them the good things: going to church and being a good guy," said Jackson, who on Sundays often brought willing players to Buck Run Baptist Church in Frankfort, Kentucky, and other churches to speak or to share their personal testimonies. "These were really good guys," she said. "At that time we had Thursday night Bible studies in the lodge. The boys could come if they wanted to. Most of them did. It was a family atmosphere. That meant so much, and I think that's the reason they still stick together. Not many months go by that I don't hear from one of them."

A fixture at the end of the bench for home and away games, Dr. Jackson often vocalized his support for the team. According to Marie, two of his favorite sayings were "Let's put the chairs in the wagon; church is out!" (which he hollered near the end of games when it became clear that Kentucky would emerge as the winner) and "How sweet it is!" (which he yelled after victories, often carving out time for a celebratory dance with the team's cheerleaders). "Our grandchildren still use his quote when we win a game," she said.

Macy remembered having peace of mind about the Jacksons' serving as houseparents: "Not only somebody to watch out for all of us, but if you got sick in the middle of the night, you didn't have to call Coach Hall; you could just go knock on [Dr. Jackson's] door. They kind of adopted all of us as their kids." He added that the lodge itself fostered a sense of pride, the notion that "you're there to play basketball as well as study, but the reason you have all these great things, this huge room, this huge bed, and all this stuff was because of your basketball scholarship. It made you want to work hard and be successful."

The lodge required certain finishing touches after the players moved in. "We had to tie our doors shut and wedge them so they wouldn't be open all the time until we got knobs," Rob Bolton said. "It was kind of fun to move in that way because we all enjoyed the fact that we were in there and that we were experiencing it brand new for the first time. It was new to the coaching staff, the university, and to the country."

As in most regular college dorms, music from FM radio stations, turntables, eight-track tape players, and cassette players was a nearly constant backdrop in Wildcat Lodge. "The players came from different cultures, different music styles," Mike Murphy recalled. "Jay Shidler was an REO Speedwagon fan. We used to played REO Speedwagon's album *You Can Tune a Piano but You Can't Tuna Fish* before every game, and everybody had their music cranked; just rockin'. Each room had its own beat."

The basement of Wildcat Lodge, pictured here in 1978, featured a recreation room that included a pool table and two pinball machines. (Courtesy of the *Lexington Herald-Leader*. Photo by Frank Anderson.)

Courts and the late Mike Phillips used to play guitar together. "He was like the rock star on our team," Courts said. "He loved Aerosmith, and he would have had his hair really long if he could have."

More than anything, the lodge provided the team with a haven to decompress from the fishbowl of UK basketball and just be a college kid. LaVon Williams would paint, make clothes, and design T-shirts to relax. Options for down time included playing spades (some games "approached the intensity of basketball practice," Tim Stephens said), shooting a game of pool, playing pinball, or just hanging out. "I just remember sitting around at night," Murphy said. "It was a different group of guys, and we'd just hang out watching the TV and just talk about life and get to know each other." To Tony Sosby, he and the other residents of Wildcat Lodge "weren't secluded, but we did sort of live in our own little world that allowed

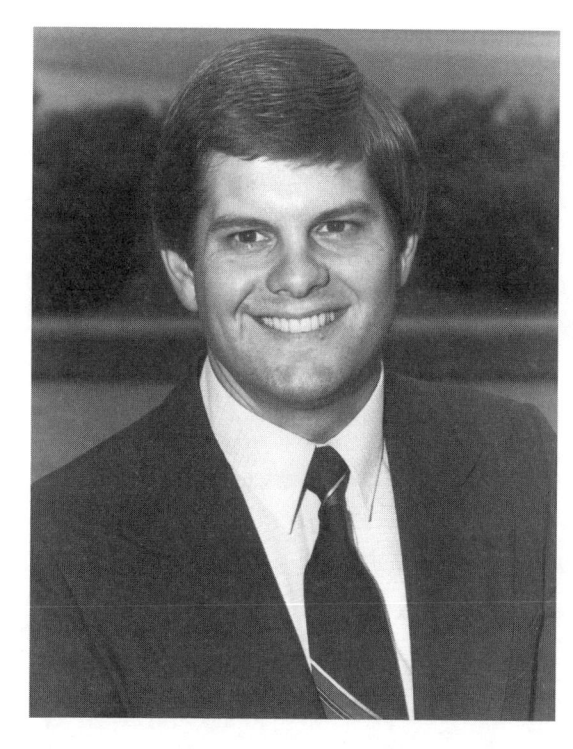

Before joining Kentucky's staff as an assistant coach in 1977, Joe Dean Jr. played guard for Mississippi State and competed against the Wildcats in the program's last official game in Memorial Coliseum on March 8, 1976. (Courtesy of the University of Kentucky Archives.)

us to think nothing but basketball and about your fellow teammates all the time. If there was something wrong, you knew it because you lived with them. It made it a better situation and more competitive situation, too."

From his apartment at the front of the dwelling, Tripp Ramsey manned a control switch to every telephone in the building. He cut off the telephone lines at curfew each night and turned them back on when he awoke the next morning. "If there was a home game and we were having quiet time in the afternoon after shoot-around, I would turn the phones off so the guys wouldn't be bothered," he said. Ramsey also accommodated requests for after-hours workouts in Memorial Coliseum. "Some of [the players] would holler at me on a Friday or Saturday when the coliseum was locked up and say, 'I wanna go shoot,' so I'd go over, open it up, turn the lights on, and whoever wanted to shoot would shoot," he said. "It was a commitment, and it was like they just weren't going to be stopped."

The night before home games, "you almost felt like a parent making sure the guys were in their own rooms," Don Sullivan said. "We'd bring them a snack around ten o'clock, usually hamburgers and milkshakes, that sort of thing. If one of them was sneaking in the backdoor at five minutes after ten o'clock, we'd just let it go." Coach Hall held a master key to the lodge and sometimes showed up unexpectedly to check on the team. "I'd be out recruiting and come in at two o'clock in the morning and check the dorm," Hall said. "I wouldn't check every kid. They never knew when I might come in."

Though Robey didn't live in Wildcat Lodge because he was married at the time, he appreciated that his teammates had their own place to call home. "When you live in a regular dormitory like we did my first three years in Holmes Hall, and you're trying to get rest the night before a Saturday ball game, that's when a lot of students are getting ready for the weekend and are up," he explained. "We had different hours. We always got up early and went in to do our workouts, and our study patterns were different than most students. I think having a facility for athletes is important because you have different hours. I think it also helps you become more team-oriented because you're around your teammates more."

There were no dedicated cooks at Wildcat Lodge during the 1978 spring semester, so the players ate most of their meals at the student center cafeteria or at Jerry's restaurant near campus. The night before home games, the team might go out somewhere in Lexington for a meal, but on game days, "we'd have a shoot-around in the morning over at Rupp, then we'd have lunch, and then a pre-game meal, maybe in the neighborhood of 3:30 to 4:00 o'clock at the student union building," Ramsey recalled. "After the game we might all go someplace to get something to eat. Jerry's was just a

Dr. V. A. Jackson celebrates with members of the Wildcat cheerleading squad after a basketball victory. (Courtesy of Marie Jackson.)

block away." During one team meal at Cliff Hagan's Ribeye steakhouse in Lexington, Truman Claytor recalled that Scott Courts devoured two sixteen-ounce steaks, two baked potatoes, a dinner salad, and a loaf of bread. "Joe B. chewed him out so bad, and the next day in practice he had to run extra," Claytor said. "I'd never seen a man eat that much steak in my life. Coach Hall had to make sure that when we had team meals there, everybody had their own basket of bread and their own bottle of steak sauce. We had a team that could eat!"

Once their games or practices ended, "we would talk life stuff, girlfriends, stuff guys normally talk about," Givens added. "We tried to be as normal as possible once we got away from the court because you need to get away from it. You can't take it with you everywhere you go. Guys had to study, and guys had other stuff going on, so there was plenty of time to be away from each other. But we usually tried to eat together because we finished practice at the same time."

Whether team members were leaving the lodge or just arriving, it wasn't uncommon to encounter fans hoping to meet them or to secure an autograph. "Sometimes there would be twenty to thirty people, hardworking blue-collar people of Kentucky who brought their kids and waited outside for hours to have an opportunity to meet us," Courts recalled. "You could just feel the responsibility when you came out the front door because a guy would say, 'I'm Bill Johnson from Danville. I brought my son because all he wants to do in the world is meet a Wildcat.' I used to take them on tours of the house once in a while. Just wonderful people. They always say that great rock bands are great because they have the greatest fans. It's true of sports, too, isn't it? Fans that won't settle for anything else but total excellence."

5

A Cold Snap and a Loss

The 1977–1978 season marked the second year that UK junior Gary Tanner served on the cheerleading squad as the university's first officially sanctioned Wildcat mascot for men's basketball and football games. To entertain spectators during time-outs and at halftime, he'd often hurl a basketball from half-court toward the goal "and probably make it six out of ten times," he said. "Someone on the athletic department staff told me, 'Don't do that anymore. You're showing the team up.'"

Tanner often drove himself to games in Rupp while wearing his faux-fur suit, and sometimes the Wildcat head also, which caught the attention of fellow drivers and their passengers en route to the arena. "To do that, I'd have to look out of one eye, which probably wasn't the smartest thing to do," he said. He'd typically lose six to eight pounds every game from performing routines with the cheerleading squad and darting up and down the steep aisles of Rupp Arena.

UK is a public university, but Coach Hall exposed his team to food for the soul by inviting Rev. David N. Blondell, senior minister of Crestwood Christian Church, Lexington, to share devotionals at

Gary Tanner (in foreground) was UK's first officially sanctioned Wildcat mascot. He debuted during the 1976–1977 academic year and entertained fans during football and basketball games. (Courtesy of the *Lexington Herald-Leader*. Photo by Frank Anderson.)

the close of every home pregame meal. He made no presumptions about the religious background of players or their spiritual beliefs. "I never prayed for wins," Blondell said. "I never prayed for things that I thought were out of the realm of what my purpose was, but I prayed for health and wholeness and fair play and good sportsmanship." He often incorporated analogies related to basketball and other sports. "I think one time I talked about a special five-member team I would have composed with five of [Christ's] disciples, and why I'd chosen certain ones for positions on that team," he said. "I talked about Peter[1] being the floor general, and how he was always the key individual or spokesperson for the team. When I was jokingly accosted for not 'pulling the team through' tough losses, I used to kid and respond as to how I was only in charge of home games. I would say, 'You notice we won more home games than we lost on the road.'" Coach Hamilton, who is currently the head men's basketball coach at Florida State University, said that Reverend Blondell's devotionals enhanced the team's moral compass. "Coach Hall was always big on the overall cultural development of the players, which I've learned and kept with me to this day," he said.

The Wildcats began 1978 with Southeastern Conference (SEC) play and a 72–59 victory against Vanderbilt at Rupp Arena on January 2. One by one they defeated more SEC opponents, including an 86–67 road win against Florida on January 7, a 101–77 road win against Auburn on January 9, and a 96–76 win in Rupp Arena against LSU on January 14. The matchup against LSU was physical, with fifty-four personal fouls called in forty minutes—thirty-one of them on the Tigers, whose roster included two Kentuckians: guard Kenny Higgs of Owensboro and forward Durand Macklin of Louisville. After the game, LSU Coach Dale Brown complained that Kentucky "was brutalizing the game of basketball" by being "too physical. They've taken away the beauty of the game. You almost can't referee against Kentucky."[2] Macklin predicted that things would go differently when the two teams faced each other the following month in Baton Rouge. "Our crowd will stimulate us, and we'll have home court advantage," he said.[3]

Next was a home game against Ole Miss on January 16, a contest the Wildcats won 76–56, led by 15 points from Lee, followed by 14 from Phillips, 13 from Givens, and 12 from Macy. These victories occurred during a month that brought persistent snow and frigid temperatures to the Bluegrass State. According to the Western Kentucky University–based Kentucky Climate Center, measurable snow fell in Kentucky on nineteen days during January 1978. The National Guard was called out to help clear roads from January 16 through 20, and again on January 25 and 26, when blizzard conditions led Kentucky State Police to close all roads except those in the very southeastern corner of the state. Public schools were shuttered for most of the month. Looking back on that cold snap, Rob Bolton marveled that none of the players injured themselves from falling on the snow and ice, especially when navigating the walk from the parking lot on High Street at the top of Patterson Street, which led steeply downhill to the rear participant entrance of then two-year-old Rupp Arena. "People used to hold onto things and onto each other coming down that hill," he said. "Nothing ever happened, thankfully, but I always thought, 'Wouldn't it have been a story if Jack Givens had broken his arm and was missed for the rest of the season?'"

After one heavy snowfall that month, Bill Keightley, who lived just outside of the Fayette County line in Nicholasville, was unable to make it into Lexington for his work as a mail carrier and the basketball team's equipment manager. Being snowed in "was driving him crazy," Bolton recalled. Frustrated, he called head student manager Don Sullivan and asked for a ride in. "If Bill wasn't in the center of everything that went on around the basketball team, he was not happy," Sullivan said. "At that time I had a '76 Cadillac, but it wasn't going to make it out there because it was too big and bulky. I barely got to Memorial Coliseum with it." So Sullivan, Bolton, and Sosby borrowed Rick Robey's four-wheel-drive Chevrolet Tahoe and headed slowly out Tates Creek Road to Keightley's Nicholasville home to pick him up. Sullivan drove. "At that time the four lanes to the road ended around Armstrong Mill, then it became a two-lane road," Bolton said. "There were bulldozers trying to clear roads because it was so bad, and they were so behind. We drove and mushed and slogged. With the windchill that day I think it was below zero, but Bill was insistent on getting in."

Not long after the guys drove past where the intersection of Man O'War Boulevard and Tates Creek Road is today, they noticed a man in the distance walking toward them. As they drove closer, they realized it was Keightley, who'd grown tired of waiting, so he'd

UK basketball equipment manager Bill Keightley, pictured here after the 1977–1978 season, provided moral support to Kentucky coaches, players, and student managers during a tenure that spanned nearly five decades. He passed away in 2008 at the age of eighty-one. (Courtesy of UK Athletics.)

Fred Cowan, a native of Sturgis, Kentucky, and a freshman during the 1977–1978 season, scored 975 points during his four-year career as a Wildcat. (Courtesy of the University of Kentucky Archives.)

started to advance toward UK on foot. "I looked over at the guys and said, 'Can you believe that?!'" Bolton said. "He had on a Kentucky windbreaker and his baseball cap, and it was below zero. His ears were red. He got in and asked, 'Where in the hell have you guys been?!'"

Mission accomplished, the guys returned to campus, and Keightley lived in the coliseum for at least a week. "He would sleep in the training room, shower in the locker room, and he'd get up and go carry the mail," Bolton said. Keightley, who became affectionately known as "Mr. Wildcat," became a father figure not only to many players but to the managers, someone to lean on when times got tough, someone to act as a sounding board while navigating college life. "Outside of my parents, I probably learned more from him at that time in my life than anybody else: how to treat people, how to develop a work ethic," George L. Fletcher recalled. "We were close. I guess all of the managers probably felt that way. He had such a work ethic. He had his mail-route schedule, so he could get up at 4:00 a.m. and sort his mail and get finished by noon so he could make practice. There were many times on road trips we'd come back and get back at twelve, one, or two in the morning, and he didn't go home. He'd stay in 'the cage,' which was the equipment room, and sleep for a couple of hours and go to work. Because of his work ethic, you just couldn't let Bill down, and because he had such a stake in the program and he loved it." Sometimes Keightley enlisted Sullivan's help to deliver mail to his route on Saturdays in order to finish on time for practice or game preparation. "He was the glue for the entire program," Sullivan said.

LaVon Williams visited Keightley in his office one day during his freshman year and noticed several boxes of candy bars stacked away. "I said, 'Bill, can I have a candy bar?' He said, 'Yeah, go ahead.' He called me Slim. I ate one and came back, and he said, 'Go ahead; take some more.' So he gave me the box. I went home and ate twenty-

Cawood Ledford, pictured at right with Coach Hall, was the radio play-by-play announcer for UK basketball for thirty-nine years before retiring in 1992. A native of Harlan, Kentucky, the beloved "Voice of the Wildcats" passed away in 2001 at the age of seventy-five. (Courtesy of UK Athletics.)

four of those candy bars, and the next day I was sick as a dog. Maybe that was his way of telling me, 'Don't eat all that candy!' He turned me off of candy; that was enough for me."

As midseason approached, the Wildcats traveled to Starkville, Mississippi, for a matchup against Mississippi State on January 21. The Wildcats won 75–65 and shot a remarkable 67.6 percent from the floor. "I've never had a game where I said nothing about taking a bad shot," Coach Hall said after the contest.[4] "The players were unselfish and were at their best working for good shots." Givens led the team with 21 points, Claytor followed with 13, Macy scored 12, and Robey chipped in 10. The Wildcats were now 14–0. Next stop on this road trip was Tuscaloosa, Alabama, for a game against the University of Alabama Crimson Tide, who were coached by Charles

Tim Stephens (31), a native of Revelo, Kentucky, passes the ball up court. (Courtesy of the University of Kentucky Archives.)

Martin "C. M." Newton, a UK alumnus who had been a reserve guard/forward on Adolph Rupp's 1951 NCAA National Championship team. Newton started three guards, which created a matchup challenge for the Wildcats.

Truman Claytor remembered how hot the locker room and arena felt prior to game time, a stark contrast to the comfortable temperatures from that morning's shoot-around. "We got there that night, and it was probably about one hundred degrees in our locker room," he said. "They turned the heat up on us. It was the oldest trick in the book! They pressed us ninety-four feet, caught us off guard, and we were sucking air. We couldn't breathe in the gym that night. It was bad." To complicate things, Macy said, the Crimson Tide's home court was made of tartan, a rubberized material that was not forgiving to the lower extremities. The team put in a long practice on that floor the day before the game. "I always felt like we were dead-legged that next day," Macy said. "We were a step-and-a-half slow. I don't think we had the energy to get over the hump. It was hot in there, too."

The Wildcats fell 78–62, and while Robey racked up 28 points, Givens scored only 6. "Back then, you didn't start three guards like you do today," Joe Dean Jr. said. "If we had one weakness it was that we weren't the quickest team. We were a big, strong, physical team and had great shooters in Shidler and Claytor and Macy. Alabama took us to the woodshed and beat us pretty good. I think that was good for the team because it was a wake-up call that 'you're not going to run the table. You've got to come to play every night, because everybody's going to give you their best shot.'"

Following the upset, Coach Newton characterized the win as "one of the biggest" in the history of Alabama basketball. "We knew we couldn't match Kentucky in size and strength, and we knew we'd have some mismatches," he said.[5] "But by using the small lineup, we created some mismatches for them, too. Their size and strength could not match our quickness."

6

Navigating the "Pressure Cooker"

Early in the season, Coach Dick Parsons knew this team was special, but the loss in Tuscaloosa caused some soul-searching. "All through that season, it's in the back of your mind that you're doing the right thing, you're still playing well, but you wonder: what do you need to do to maintain the right focus?" he said. "This team was a little stale in the latter part of the season."

Lexington dentist Roy Holsclaw said that during a late-January postgame radio interview show, Coach Hall lamented how year after year his teams fell into a shooting slump and struggled to maintain stamina and sharpness by the time late January and February rolled around. A local physician who listened to the radio show that night wrote a letter to Coach Hall, suggesting that the symptoms he described indicated possible depletion of potassium, a key electrolyte that impacts energy and stamina. "He wrote, 'I would suggest that you put your players on a high-potassium diet,'" Dr. Holsclaw recalled. "Coach Hall handed me the letter and said, 'Roy, why don't you check into this.'"

Chemical examination of blood drawn from the players revealed that some did have low potassium levels, so Dr. Holsclaw conferred with the physician, who recommended adding potassium-rich pineapples, bananas, and strawberries to their diet. Coincidentally, Dr. Holsclaw's wife, Katharine, had a frozen-dessert recipe handed down from her mother that contained all of those fruits in their natural juices, so the couple mixed up the recipe in a three-gallon Tupperware container and stuck it in their freezer at home. Dr. Holsclaw brought in the frozen treat prior to many practices and all remaining home games that season, intended for the players to consume afterward. "I would turn it over to one of the managers," he said. "They'd set it on a counter or something, and during the two-hour course of the practice or game it would thaw out partially, and we'd serve it in a little plastic cup." The concoction became known as Wildcat Slush.[1] "It seemed to give us a boost," Coach Parsons said.

Recipe for Wildcat Slush
2 cups of sugar
1 cup of water
Boil until the sugar dissolves, then let it cool.
1 20-ounce can of crushed pineapple
1 12-ounce can of frozen orange juice
1 12-ounce glass of water
5 fresh bananas, sliced
1 quart thawed frozen strawberries
Mix ingredients, and freeze in your container of choice. Remove container from freezer and serve when mixture turns slushy.
(Recipe courtesy of Katharine Holsclaw.)

That a Lexington couple felt compelled to help the Wildcats in this way might seem unusual to an outsider, but to Kentucky residents and to the global fan base known as Big Blue Nation, such a gesture comes as no surprise. Devotion to the program runs bone-deep, and people from all walks of life long to be a part of it. Maybe that's why a sense of unrelenting pressure connects UK basketball players and coaches from team to team and era to era. Pressure to represent the university and the Commonwealth well. Pressure to do their part to see that UK maintains its lead as the winningest program in college basketball history. Pressure to ensure that the bar for excellence and discipline set decades ago by Adolph Rupp remains high. They also face pressure from fans, some of whom expect the Wildcats to reach the Final Four every year. As current Coach John Calipari told *Sporting News* in 2012,[2] "You're under a microscope [at UK]. Some of the stuff that goes on in other places cannot go on here. Just, you can't. Players can't hide here on the basketball court. There's no rock, there's no crack big enough. You've got to be able to play."

It was like that in the late 1970s, too. "We were in this pressure cooker," Scott Courts said. "I'd go on a date, and the girl would talk about how my first step could have been quicker. All [of] these people with all this basketball knowledge, collectively pressuring us to win. The expectations were immense. The pressure was so intense that we all huddled or hid out in the basketball house, supporting each other. Winning wasn't enough. If we didn't win by a wide margin, a majority of fans would feel like we lost the game. Perfection was a constant expectation."

Sometimes, getting away from campus was the best way for players to escape from the spotlight. "People would hound them to death sometimes," Ralph Hacker recalled. Givens and Lee visited their families in Lexington for meals. Robey's hideaway of choice was Claiborne Farm, where he worked during the summers. "I'd go out and spend time with the Hancocks and have a meal out there, just to get away from all of the commotion going on in Lexington," he said. One of Macy's outlets was babysitting Ralph and Marilyn

LaVon Williams (52) outmaneuvers Georgia's Walter Daniels for a rebound in Rupp Arena on January 30, 1978. (Courtesy of the *Lexington Herald-Leader*. Photo by David Perry.)

Hacker's daughter, Heather. "He would call up and ask, 'What are you and Marilyn doing tonight?'" Hacker recalled. "'Nothing.' He'd say, 'You and Marilyn are going out. I'm coming to babysit.' He'd bring a date, come out and watch TV, and babysit for us."

With pressure comes responsibility. Joe Dean Jr. remembered the inordinate number of basketballs and other items the team signed after practice in Memorial Coliseum during the 1977–1978 season. Bill Keightley and the managers set up a line of chairs outside of Keightley's office, and the coaches and players would sign balls and other items for about an hour and a half—an exercise that was the brainchild of Coach Hall. "One of the things he did was to make sure that if you sent a ball or a hat or a poster in and requested Kyle Macy or the entire team to sign it, it got done, and it got sent back to you," Dean said. "I find that remarkable. Coach Hall made people realize that we are a team of the people. He believed that the people in the state of Kentucky owned that program, and he wanted them to feel a part of it."

After returning from the season's first loss in Tuscaloosa, UK hosted three consecutive home games. The first was a matchup against Georgia on January 30, which UK won 90–73. Four Wildcats scored in double figures, led by 19 from Givens, then 18 each from Macy and Lee, and 11 from Robey to go along with his 14 rebounds. Next was a February 4 contest with Florida. According to a news report on the game,[3] the Wildcats were being outrebounded by a shorter Gators squad in the first half and were tied 36–36 at halftime, despite 18 points from Macy. The sophomore guard continued his strong play in the second half, however, and helped UK pull away to an 88–61 victory. By the end of the game, Macy had connected on 11 of 13 shots from the floor, plus 8 free throws, for 30 points. Three of his teammates scored in double figures, including 14 each from Givens and Lee and 12 from Phillips, who also collected 10 rebounds.

On February 6 Kentucky hosted the Auburn Tigers, who trailed by just 5 points at halftime, 45–40. However, UK opened up the second half on a 10–0 run, led by Lee and Givens, who scored 25 and 22 points, respectively, and grabbed 8 and 9 rebounds each, helping the Wildcats secure a 104–81 victory. Robey also had a strong performance, with 21 points and 10 rebounds. Macy added 17 points and 4 rebounds, while Phillips chipped in 12 points and 9 rebounds.

Next was a road trip to the Assembly Center in Baton Rouge for a February 11 rematch with LSU. Coach Hamilton remembered a rowdy atmosphere that day, from the rocks thrown at the team bus when it pulled up to the arena to the drama that unfolded when LSU's costumed tiger mascot was lowered from the rafters onto the basketball court with a long rope shortly before tip-off. "The frickin' place was in a total frenzy," he said.

Looking to avenge their 20-point loss to the Wildcats the previous month, LSU hung on to win 95–94 in overtime, even though four of their five starters fouled out in regulation, and the fifth did so in overtime. The Tigers shot 61 percent from the floor, and the Wildcats shot a respectable 56 percent, but LSU outrebounded 41–29. The Kentuckians Higgs and Macklin combined for 34 points. "The game was kind of strange because we were up in part of the first half, no problem," Fred Cowan said. "Then all of a sudden, it seemed like something came over the whole team. It's the first time I'd seen it as a player. We just got in slow motion in the second half."

Coach Hamilton's own scouting report on the Tigers backfired. "Guys were throwing up jump shots who had never shot them [before], and they were going in," he said. "I mean, they were throwing up shots that I was saying, 'What in the world is going on?' They were making shots from the parking lot. They were so hyped up, and the game meant so much, they played beyond their talent level. It was that type of atmosphere. Kentucky brought those kinds of emotions out of every team that we played."

Meanwhile, LSU Coach Dale Brown praised his counterpart. "After the game, Joe Hall shook my hand with a smile," he was quoted as saying.[4] "That takes character especially when the opposing coach had been critical of his team's style. And the [UK] president (Otis Singletary) told me he was proud of Kentucky and said we deserved to win."

One day after the loss, Coach Hall labeled his team the "Folding Five."[5] Givens remembered that he and the other seniors called a team meeting to regroup. "It was up to us to get ourselves and the team back to playing how we knew we could play," he said. "We made sure that we understood we had to get back to fundamentals. Our defense hadn't been as good. We knew we had to get back to playing the way we were capable of playing. I never want to say a loss is good for you, but every now and then you can learn more from a loss than you can from a win." Tim Stephens, who hit two jumpers out of the left corner in that game, said the loss made the team more determined. "I remember thinking, 'It's not the end of the world; we're gonna bounce back,'" he said. "I think we kind of needed that. It wasn't a fact of losing focus. I felt like we just needed to reassure ourselves and maybe try to alleviate some of the pressure we may have been putting on ourselves."

Despite the players' perspective on the loss, some Kentucky fans chose to worry. "Some fans just thought it was the end of the world that we lost that game," Don Sullivan said. "It was like the whole season was a failure. Their expectations are just amazing."

Two days later, the players faced a matchup in Oxford, Mississippi, with Ole Miss. Prior to leaving the team's hotel for an afternoon shoot-around on the Rebels' home court, Fred Cowan, Dwane Casey, and LaVon Williams were watching an episode of *Sanford and Son* on TV and realized they had just a few minutes to board the team bus outside. "We were cutting it close and ran down to get on the bus," Cowan recalled. "Coach Hall was already on the bus, so we

Kyle Macy connects on a free throw following a technical foul against Tennessee in Rupp Arena on February 15, 1978. (Courtesy of UK Athletics.)

knew we were in trouble, because he was always the last person on the bus when we traveled. Dwane reached for the door, but Coach Hall told the driver to shut the door, and they drove off. Then we hit the panic button." A sports reporter watched the incident unfold, so he drove the trio of Wildcats to the Rebeldome arena in his own car—and arrived before the team bus did.

Looking back now, Casey said that he grew to appreciate Coach Hall's penchant for discipline. "It helped make me the man I am today," said Casey, who is currently head coach of the NBA's Toronto Raptors. "At that time in your life you really didn't understand why he was tough, but now, even in the NBA, I make sure our guys are on time. If they're not there when the bus leaves, we go off and leave them, and they get fined. A lot of that is the same thing we did at Kentucky."

According to Tony Sosby, it took a while for the coaches, players, and managers to shake off the loss at LSU. During the Ole Miss game, "everybody was uptight," he said. "Coach Hall was subbing left and right, trying to send a message." At one point, Coach Hall took Macy out of the game and began to chew him out as he sat on the bench. Whatever he'd done to draw Coach Hall's ire "was very minor," recalled Sosby, who was close friends with Macy. "I know Joe B. was sending a message, but at the time I was behind the bench, leaning over to give Kyle a cup of water. I got emotionally involved, and my first thought was, 'I'm gonna throw this cup of water at Coach! I'm gonna throw it in his face!' I didn't. After I gave Kyle the water, I came back down to the end of the bench and told Mr. Keightley, 'If I do that again, I'm going to get in trouble because I'm gonna throw water on Coach Hall!' In my mind Joe B. was way out of line. I'd never heard him get on Kyle before."

Dean also remembered a revolving door of substitutions at Ole Miss—17 in the first half alone.[6] "Every time a kid made a mistake, Coach Hall took him out of the game right away," Dean said. "It didn't matter what you did. If you traveled, you came out. If you gave up a defensive play, you came out. If you threw the ball away, you came out. If you missed a shot, you came out." The Wildcats won 64–52, but it was an unsteady performance even though the team shot 52 percent from the field and outrebounded the Rebels 37–29.[7] "It was kind of ugly," Dean said. "After the game, Jack Givens was interviewed and was asked, 'How did you feel about what Coach Hall was doing during the game?' He said, 'Well, it's hard to get into rhythm when you're running in and out all the time.' That's about as critical as Jack Givens would get with anybody." (In a newspaper interview later that season, Givens's sister Barbara marveled at her brother's coolheaded demeanor on and off the court. "I've never seen him get mad," she said.[8] "I don't know how he keeps it all inside.")

The team returned to Lexington for a three-game home stand, the first against the Tennessee Volunteers on February 15. The Vols

After a defeat at Alabama on January 23, 1978, Kentucky avenged its loss with a 97–84 victory over the Crimson Tide in Rupp Arena on February 20. (Courtesy of UK Athletics.)

entered that contest after having won five straight matchups against UK, but this squad snapped that streak with a 90–77 victory led by Robey, who poured in 18 points and grabbed 8 rebounds. Four other Wildcats scored in double figures that night: Lee with 17, Macy with 13, and Claytor and Aleksinas with 10 each. During the second half, someone threw two oranges onto the court, an indication of the rivalry between these two programs. The second orange narrowly missed striking Kentucky student manager John Kinney, who was tasked with cleaning up the mess left on the court from the first orange thrown. "When it hit the floor, juice splattered in my face," Kinney recalled. "I was just thankful that I didn't get hit in the head by an orange, or it probably would have knocked me out. I would have been on national TV, knocked out in the middle of the floor."

Three days later the Wildcats tipped off against a pesky Mississippi State team, which led 56–54 with just over three minutes left in regulation.[9] Then UK's senior cocaptains went to work. First, Givens connected on a jump shot that drew a foul from Bulldog shooting guard Wiley Peck, which he turned into a three-point play to give the Wildcats a 57–56 lead. Robey sealed the victory by sinking one of two free throws he earned by taking a charge from Peck. The final score was 58–56. Givens and Macy both had 14 points, and Claytor added 10.

On February 20, UK hosted the Crimson Tide. Givens, who was held to just 6 points in the earlier loss at Tuscaloosa, avenged that performance by scoring 22 points and grabbing 4 rebounds. The Wildcats prevailed 97–84, and four of his teammates scored in double figures: Robey with 18, Macy with 15, Lee with 13, and Phillips with 11. "They're back now, and I think they'll stay back," Coach Hall said after the game.[10] "I feel good about the rest of our season."

Coach Hall's intuition was right. The team returned to the road, first to Knoxville for a February 25 rematch with Tennessee. For the first time since 1972 the Wildcats beat the Volunteers on their home court by a score of 68–57, led by 18 points from Givens, 13 from Phillips, and 13 from Robey. It was an impressive victory, considering that many members of the team had being ailing from a bout with the flu for several days leading up to the contest. "We had players who couldn't even get out of bed—they had to have their meals sent to them," Coach Hall said after the game.[11] Next was a trip to Athens, Georgia, for a February 27 contest against the Bulldogs. According to the *Sunday Herald-Leader,* Kentucky jumped out to a 20–12 lead with 12:27 left in the first half and by halftime had stretched the lead to 19 points, 46–27.[12] Georgia cut into that lead in the second half but fell to UK 78–67, earning the Wildcats a record of 23–2 and the 1978 SEC title. Givens and Robey led the way with 15 points apiece, while Claytor scored 12 (all in the first half), and Macy added 10, along with 10 assists.

Next was the final regular-season game at Rupp, a March 4 nationally televised matchup with the up-tempo University of

The final regular-season game in Rupp Arena against UNLV marked "Senior Night" for Kentucky's four seniors. Standing at midcourt for the national anthem prior to tip-off are, from left, Kyle Macy, seniors Jack Givens, Mike Phillips, James Lee, Rick Robey, and Wildcats mascot Gary Tanner. (Courtesy of the *Lexington Herald-Leader*. Photo by E. Martin Jessee.)

Nevada Las Vegas Runnin' Rebels, who were coached by the late Jerry Tarkanian and featured star players Reggie Theus and Tony Smith. It was also Senior Night, a time to honor Givens, Robey, Phillips, and Lee, for suiting up in blue and white for four years. "It's sad to think when basketball time arrives next winter, we won't be watching the 'Goose' sailing one of those velvet-smooth jumpers through the nets, or Rick Robey driving with reckless abandon for a three-point play or Mike Phillips wheeling and driving up a hook shot or James Lee roaring down the court for one of his patented slam dunks," Oscar Combs wrote in *The Cats' Pause* that week.[13] "It just won't be the same." On Senior Night the foursome threw down 7 dunks during the game: 3 by Robey, 2 by Lee, and 1 each by Givens and Phillips. It was a tight contest in the first half, with UK up by only one point at halftime, but the Wildcats pulled away

Rick Robey scores during the "Senior Night" matchup against UNLV at Rupp Arena. (Courtesy of UK Athletics.)

in the second half and rolled to a 92–70 victory. They shot 64.5 percent from the floor and outrebounded the Runnin' Rebels 38–13. "Kentucky does everything well," Tarkanian said after the game.[14] "Robey was just sensational. God, just sensational. We tried everyone on him, even Theus, but there was no stopping him." Robey led UK with 26 points, followed by 24 from Givens, 13 from Lee, and 10 from Claytor. Phillips added 7 points and pulled down 9 rebounds. "I knew after that game that we were back, focused, and doing the things we needed to do to be able to move forward and win the title," Robey recalled. "All four of us really played well, and it seemed like we all meshed. We beat a very good team soundly that night. Throughout the year, one really good thing about this team was that every night somebody stepped up. We all knew each other's roles. We knew how to get the ball to certain people in certain positions to where they could capitalize. We knew each other's strengths and weaknesses really well."

For the last game of the regular season, the players traveled to Nashville for a March 6 contest with Vanderbilt. UK connected on 60 percent of its shots on its way to a 78–68 victory. Macy scored 22 points, followed by 8 from Givens. The team also set a new UK men's basketball record in field-goal percentage during a season: 53.8 percent, which bested the old record of 50.6 percent set by the 1971 Wildcats.[15]

7

Tourney Time

The 1978 NCAA Men's Basketball Tournament Selection Committee assigned thirty-two teams to compete in one of four geographic regions. The Mideast Region included Kentucky, which was ranked number one in the final regular-season Associated Press (AP) poll; the number-three-ranked Marquette Warriors[1] and their star point guard, Butch Lee, the prevailing NCAA champions; and the number-six-ranked Michigan State Spartans and their freshman standout guard-forward, Earvin "Magic" Johnson. The West Region featured UCLA (ranked number two in the final regular-season AP poll), Arkansas (number seven), Kansas (number nine), and North Carolina (number eleven). The Midwest Region showcased DePaul (number four), Notre Dame (number ten), Louisville (number twelve), and Houston (number fourteen); while the East Region included Duke (number eight) and unranked Indiana and Villanova.

In the first round of NCAA Tournament play on March 11 in Knoxville, Tennessee, UK faced the Florida State University Seminoles, who were ranked number thirteen in the final regular-season AP poll. Prior to game time, Coach Hall wrote the number "200"

90 FORTY MINUTES TO GLORY

In the first round of NCAA Tournament play, the Wildcats matched up against Florida State in Knoxville, Tennessee, on March 11. Pictured is the cover of the program sold at the event. (Courtesy of Don Sullivan.)

on a blackboard in the locker room and told the team that's how many minutes of playing time were left in order to bring a fifth NCAA crown back to Lexington. He recalled no specific inspiration for the gesture: "It just hit me," he said. Panic set in as the upset-minded Seminoles built a 7-point lead at halftime, 39–32. Bolton remembered conferring with Sosby, wondering if this would be the end of an otherwise remarkable season for the heavily favored Wildcats. "We started to talk to each other [and wonder] if it was too late to go on spring break," he said. "Florida State through that first half was faster, stronger, [and] they were getting every 50-50 ball."

Coach Hall was furious at his starting five, "perturbed by the way they were lollygagging around, weren't playing defense," he said. The Seminoles "were getting run-outs on us. We just weren't alert. We had so much more talent than they did, and they were just out-hustling us." During halftime, Hall told his players, "I'm not gonna let you guys lose this game; I'll lose it myself. I'll sit you down to let the subs lose it." He benched Robey, Claytor, and Givens for reserve players LaVon Williams, Fred Cowan, and Dwane Casey, hoping they'd provide a spark when the second half tipped off. He left Macy and Phillips in. "I told Dick Parsons when we left the locker room at halftime, 'Dickie, if this doesn't work, we're not going back to Lexington; we'll go to Florida and go fishing.'"

Cowan couldn't believe that he was asked to start the second half. "At first I thought, 'Did I just hear my name? Was he really talking to me?' I thought, 'He's not going to stick subs in there. The game is too important.'" Lee was also dumbfounded. "Jack [Givens] and I were sitting next to each other and I said, 'We have to catch a ride home because he's not going to let us get on the bus. Neither are the fans.' That was a tough call by Coach Hall. That was one of the gutsiest and most remarkable moves."

The coaching maneuver caught Williams off guard as well. "I was thinking, 'Man, if we lose this game, I'm going home to Florida to see my grandfather,'" he said. "But something hit me then. I realized Coach was depending on everybody to give us a kick-start. He went to the sixth, seventh, and eighth man off the bench." Once

Assistant Coach Dick Parsons (center) is flanked by Kentucky's towering big men. Pictured from left are Scott Courts, Chuck Aleksinas, Mike Phillips, and Rick Robey. (Courtesy of Dick Parsons.)

the second half started, "a feeling came over me like I knew we were going to win the championship," Williams said. "We just couldn't lose."

When Florida State coach Hugh Durham saw the new second-half lineup, "my reaction . . . was that when you play the other team's support troops it's time to build a lead and take the momentum," he said after the game.[2] "But they have more depth than we do, and it's amazing how much more tired you get when you're behind than when you're ahead."

Coach Hall's strategy worked. For about the first ten minutes of the second half, the reserves, along with Macy and Phillips, slowed down the Seminoles' offense. When the starters returned they went on a 14–0 run to reverse a 53–48 deficit into a 62–53 lead with 6:53 left in regulation.[3] "They just went to war," Hall said. The Wildcats prevailed, 85–76. Williams called the victory "probably the greatest game Coach Hall coached." Macy characterized his coach's gamble as "kind of the shock treatment. When [the starters] got back in we got focused, went on a run, and were able to win. I think every team during the course of a championship run has a game where you have to overcome something, whether it's adversity, or to have a little luck."

The victory earned UK a trip to Dayton, Ohio, for the NCAA Mideast Regional and a March 16 matchup against the unranked Miami University Redskins,[4] who had upended Marquette. Before a crowd of more than 13,400, UK cruised to a 91–69 victory led by senior Mike Phillips, who scored a season-high 24 points and grabbed 4 rebounds. Four of his teammates also scored in double figures: Robey with 14, Claytor with 13, and Givens and Lee with 12 each. The Wildcats outrebounded the Redskins 37–24. After the victory, Coach Hall was quoted as saying that his team "was in a tournament frame of mind. We played better defense tonight than we have the last part of the season, and that was a big, big factor in our win."[5] The Cats were now 120 minutes of playing time closer to a national championship.

Next was a March 18 matchup in Dayton against Michigan State, with the winner advancing to the NCAA Division I Men's Basketball Championship. According to Dwane Casey, prior to tip-off, Coach Hall joked with his team about Earvin Johnson's nickname. "Coach said, 'Can you believe they have a guy who calls himself "Magic"? Who in the heck calls themselves "Magic"?' Michigan State had a really good team, well coached by Jud Heathcote, just very good all-around." The Spartans led early in the game and were up 27–22 at halftime. "They had one of the toughest 2–3 zones I'd ever seen in my life," Claytor said. "They forced Kyle and me out a little farther."

Longtime broadcast partners Cawood Ledford (left) and Ralph Hacker call a Wildcats game. Seated to Hacker's left is Rick Bailey, former staff writer for the *Lexington Herald-Leader*. (Courtesy of UK Athletics.)

Prior to the start of the second half, Coach Hall and Coach Hamilton huddled with Macy and Robey courtside as their teammates finished warm-ups. Coach Hamilton had devised a strategy to run against the Spartans' matchup zone meant to free up Macy for jump shots, so he and Coach Hall discussed the play in front of UK's bench. "Coach Hamilton was saying, 'Throw it here, and then, Robey, you come off the pick. Jack will be here, and Mike will slide here, so if you don't have a shot here, this guy will be open,'" Macy said. "They drew up the play right as the buzzer sounded to start the second half. It worked to perfection. [The Spartans] didn't have an answer. I either got a shot, or they'd foul me coming off a screen. It was a good halftime adjustment."

Early in the second half, Kentucky switched from a man-to-man defense to a 1-3-1 zone, which slowed the Spartans' offense. Macy went on to score 18 points in the game—10 of them free throws. Six of those free throws came in the final 2:43 of play and

Jack Givens defends Michigan State University freshman guard Earvin "Magic" Johnson (33), who was held to six points in Kentucky's 52–49 victory over the Spartans at the NCAA Mideast Regional in Dayton, Ohio. (Courtesy of the Michigan State University Archives and Historical Collections.)

helped to seal a 52–49 victory for the Wildcats, earning Macy Most Valuable Player honors after the final buzzer sounded. "Macy was one of the best free-throw shooters in the country," Claytor recalled.

"In practice, we'd have to shoot 30 free throws every day, and the managers would keep track. Some days I'd go 26 for 30. One day I overheard one of the managers say, 'He [Kyle] hasn't missed in about four weeks.' You know how many free throws that is? You're shooting 30 free throws a day, and this guy has gone a whole month."

Earvin Johnson, who was defended by Givens, scored just 6 points in the contest, even though he had averaged 17 points per game that year. "In going to that 1-3-1 zone, they clogged up the middle," Johnson said after the game.[6] "We're the type of team that likes to penetrate, and we had to shoot over them. To make matters worse, the ball wasn't dropping."

Givens chipped in 14 points, and Phillips added 10 points and 8 rebounds. After the win, Coach Hall gave a nod to the senior leadership. "This senior class has done a lot," he said.[7] "Go to the Final Four, win the NIT. There's one thing left."

In a 1996 audio interview, Bill Keightley reflected on the team's bus trip from Dayton back to Lexington after the victory, which earned UK a trip to the Final Four for the second time in four years. "The closer we got back to Lexington—I'm talking about when we crossed the Ohio River—on every overpass on the interstate there [were] people standing on the overpasses with banners and signs and waving, and the closer you got to Lexington, the bigger the crowds," Keightley said.[8]

"You would have thought it was the funeral for John F. Kennedy coming on a train headed to Washington or something," Gettelfinger added. "Every bridge and every side street and everything on that road [were] lit up with Kentucky fans." Drivers passing the team bus were "honking all the way from the Kentucky line back to Lexington."

These Wildcats were eighty game minutes from a national crown.

8

Meet Me in St. Louis

Two days before the team was to leave for the Final Four at the Checkerdome in St. Louis, Scott Courts heard a gentle knock on the door to his room in Wildcat Lodge. It was Dr. Jackson, who walked in, opened the window blinds, and sat on the side of his bed.

"He held my hand and said, 'Son, I've got some bad news for you,'" said Courts, who remembered looking out the dorm window to watch the sunrise.

"I said, 'Dr. Jackson, my father died, didn't he?' My father had suffered a devastating heart attack about a week earlier.

"He said, 'Yes, son. Your father died.'

"The next thing I knew I was on a jet to go spend a day with my mother in Colorado, and then I landed in St. Louis and walked into a crowded hotel lobby and 'boom,' I was there. It was manic."

Courts referred to the Jacksons as "great spiritual advisers" during his time at UK. "There wasn't anyone on that team that wasn't a spiritual or moral leader," he added. "We were driven by the force of discipline, morality, and spirit. There was no question about that; it was almost a divine mission. There wasn't anyone on that team that didn't conduct themselves within those boundaries.

The Checkerdome, pictured here in 1979, hosted the NCAA Division I Men's Basketball Championship in 1973 and in 1978. It was demolished in 1992. (Courtesy The State Historical Society of Missouri-George McCue Photograph Collection.)

It sounds ridiculous, but it was an immense experience, to have that kind of discipline."

The four Wildcat seniors knew a thing or two about preparing for a Final Four, so they set the tone with their teammates. "Our freshman year out in San Diego, we did everything sightseeing-wise you could as a team," recalled Robey, referring to the 1975 Final Four. "I shouldn't say that we weren't there to not win it, but we were just kind of happy to be there. This time, we were happy to be there, but we were on a mission to win it. I think we just had a little bit of a different feeling going into that Final Four, because it was Jack's, James's, Mike's, and my last shot at it. We tried to stay more focused while we were there instead of enjoying all the hoopla."

Truman Claytor remembered Robey and the other seniors describing the journey to St. Louis as a business trip. "Rick, Jack, Mike, and James told us exactly how it was going to be: 'Don't get

A photo of Jack Givens in action against North Carolina appeared on the cover of the NCAA's 1978 Championship program. (Courtesy of Kevin Cook.)

involved in all the distractions; we're out here to win this thing,'" he said. "I was so excited just to go. We weren't just going out there happy to be in the Final Four; we were there to win it."

Once the team arrived in the city known as the Gateway to the

West, Coach Hall "tried to keep a stern level of attitude on everything: not too high, not too low," Macy recalled. When a team makes it to the Final Four, "the lights are brighter; it's so different," Coach Parsons added. "You try to shelter your kids, you try to go up back steps, and you try to get to your pregame meals. You certainly wouldn't want to walk through the hotel lobby. We would take back stairwells just to try to keep things on an even pace, but you can't do it because it takes on a seriousness that you sometimes can't control. But it didn't bother this team. They were just so tough mentally along with the way they played that it just didn't seem like the lights were all that brighter."

The Wildcats were enjoying their first team meal in the host hotel when word came that Jay Shidler's mother was seriously ill in a hospital in Vincennes, Indiana, located about 154 miles east of St. Louis. Coach Hall suggested finding someone to fly Shidler to Vincennes on a twin-engine plane, but Ramsey said that because of strong, persistent winds that day, he'd be hard-pressed to find a willing pilot. "This is bad," Ramsey told him. "Plus, I'll get caught air sick, and Jay will get air sick. This is not going to be good." As an alternative, a Kentucky state trooper chauffeured Shidler to Vincennes by car. Ramsey went along. After arriving at the hospital, Shidler spent about five hours with his mother, who had been admitted for an overdose of Valium. "She had struggled with the separation from my father two years prior [and] had not been in a good frame of mind," Shidler said. "Doctors felt it was a suicide attempt because of the amount ingested. She stated it was an accident, so we never really knew for sure. We were just thankful we didn't lose her at that time." When it became apparent that she was going to be okay, Shidler, Ramsey, and the trooper returned to St. Louis and arrived in the wee morning hours of game day against the Arkansas Razorbacks, Kentucky's first opponent in the national semifinals. "She was fine and was able to watch the game," he said of his mother. "I didn't get much sleep the night before, but you do what you got

James Lee (32) puts up a shot during the 1978 NCAA Championship Semifinal game between UK and Arkansas. (Courtesy of the *Lexington Herald-Leader.* Photo by Frank Anderson.)

to do. The game was probably therapeutic, to get my mind off of it for a couple of hours."

The Checkerdome,[1] an indoor arena that opened in 1929, was the site of the 1973 NCAA Men's Basketball Final Four, and it served as home to numerous sports franchises before being demolished in 1999. Previous tenants included the St. Louis Hawks of the National Basketball Association, the Spirits of St. Louis of the American Basketball Association, the St. Louis Blues of the National Hockey League, and the Saint Louis Billikens men's basketball team. The 1977–1978 Arkansas Razorbacks, meanwhile, were coached by Eddie Sutton[2] and ranked seventh in the AP poll going into NCAA Tournament play. Coach Parsons brought along game film of Arkansas playing Memphis earlier that season, but he expressed concern with Coach Hall about viewing it with the team in St. Louis. "Arkansas was probably the best team in the nation at that time," Parsons said. "They had three guys that were good [NBA] draft choices. Arkansas made 15 straight field goals to start the game [against Memphis]. I told Coach Hall, 'I don't want to show this film.' He said, 'Why?' I said, 'Well, Arkansas's pretty darn good. I don't want them to have any apprehension about the game. We can win the game with our bench and with our strength.' That's the only time I remember not showing a game film of the opposing team."

Robey had his own inkling that Arkansas "was going to be our toughest matchup, because they had the triplets in [Sidney] Moncrief, [Marvin] Delph, and [Ron] Brewer, and they were all very good players."[3]

A crowd of 18,721 gathered to watch the Wildcats and Razorbacks battle for a spot in the title game. The semifinals and finals were played on Indiana University's home basketball court. The Checkerdome's own basketball court contained dead spots, so the NCAA decided to transport the Hoosiers' portable home floor from Bloomington.[4]

Jack Givens (21) defends Sidney Moncrief of Arkansas. (Courtesy of the *Lexington Herald-Leader*. Photo by Frank Anderson.)

The Arkansas triplets' hopes of upending UK were dashed, thanks in large part to the senior duo of Givens and Lee. Givens scored 23 points on 10 for 16 shooting from the field, including a fast-break basket that put his team ahead 63–59 with 1:43 in regulation, while Lee added 13 points and pulled down 8 rebounds. According to Coach Parsons, the fast-break basket was called a "home-run play where Givens would screen for the guard and come out of that screen and sprint to the other end. The guard would throw the long pass, a Hail Mary pass. He got behind their defenders. On this particular play Macy threw the inbounds pass to Jack, and he scored. The well-executed play sealed the victory for the Cats."

The Wildcats prevailed, 64–59. "In our matchups defensively, Arkansas presented some problems for us, but I think our size and ability to play together enabled us to win that game," said Robey, who scored 8 points and pulled down 8 rebounds in the contest.

Kyle Macy (4) puts up a jump shot against the Razorbacks. (Courtesy of the *Lexington Herald-Leader*. Photo by Frank Anderson.)

After the game, Moncrief was quoted as saying that "all you ever hear about is Kentucky's physical strength and about how they beat up on everybody. But they're not like that at all. You've got to realize that they're a very good basketball team, not just that they're big and strong. They have very adequate quickness."[5] Although the Wildcats won by just 5 points, Ralph Hacker remembered that Kentucky outplayed Arkansas in all aspects of the game. "Later on, when Eddie Sutton became coach at Kentucky, he said, 'That may have been the toughest game I ever coached in my life. Those guys were not gonna let us win that ball game.'"

Defeating the Razorbacks earned the Wildcats a coveted spot in the championship game, but you wouldn't have known it. According to Hacker, there was no jumping up and down. No screaming and hollering. No chants of "We're number one" while waving index fingers in the air. "It was a business day," he said. Coach Hall offered the players an opportunity to decompress for dinner and perhaps a movie that evening, but Robey proposed a different idea: stay in the hotel and watch a replay of the Notre Dame–Duke game to prepare for a championship matchup with the Blue Devils. "That's how intense they were, and that's the kind of concentration we had all year long," Coach Parsons said. "That's a pretty good indicator of how they were thinking. They didn't want to leave any stone unturned." Robey said that his suggestion was meant to keep the team focused on what brought them to St. Louis in the first place. "We only had forty-eight hours and our careers were over, so we needed to zero in on why we were there for these next forty-eight hours," he said. "If we did what we were supposed to do, we were going to enjoy it. I felt very confident that with our experience, once we got to that game, I felt like we were going to win it."

The next morning, NCAA officials hosted an Easter Sunday press conference with representatives from both teams. The UK contingent included Coach Hall, Robey, Macy, Phillips, and Shidler. Macy recalled that the Duke players "had gotten to bed early, and they were all relaxed and goofing off. We were still half asleep by the time we came to the press conference, so we weren't nearly as cheer-

Coach Hall (far right) speaks during a press conference on the day before the championship game against Duke. Seated to Hall's right are Truman Claytor, Rick Robey, the press conference moderator, and Jay Shidler. (Courtesy of UK Athletics.)

ful." After all, he continued, Kentucky's semifinal game against Arkansas the prior night had "started late, so by the time we were done and got something to eat, it took us a while to unwind and go to sleep. That was the storyline the media was going to go with: Duke was having fun, and we weren't being able to enjoy it."

In an article[6] that included remarks made at the press conference, Bill Jauss of the *Chicago Tribune* described Robey, his teammates, and Coach Hall as "a grim-looking tight-lipped bunch on Easter Sunday." During the event, Robey offered his take on the perception that the Wildcats were too serious-minded to have fun. "You can't enjoy things during the hard grind of the season," he explained. "To be successful, you can't enjoy things during work time."

Coach Hall was quoted in the article as saying that "so much was expected of this team. We ranked No. 1 almost all season. This team has gone all season without a celebration."

That was about to change.

9

Forty Minutes to Glory

Before Kentucky's morning practice on championship game day, March 27, an impromptu players-only meeting transpired in the Checkerdome locker room before the coaches arrived. "I can remember Jack saying, 'Mike, you know Coach Hall's going to be on you. Just don't pay attention. Just go out there and play your game,'" Macy said. "I remember thinking, 'This is the national championship game, and you're saying don't listen to your coach?' But they were experienced. Coach liked to jump on Mike Phillips. At times, Mike would react instead of focusing on the game. That says something about the experience and maturity of that team. They were saying, 'Filter the stuff. Don't take it personally. Let it go, and just play your game.'"

Reverend Blondell had not planned to be a spectator for the championship game, but a friend who attended the semifinals called him on March 26 to say he'd secured three extra tickets for the event, so early the next morning Blondell drove the five-plus hours from Lexington with a fellow minister and a parishioner to attend. Mindful of his opportunity to serve up one more devotional, he crafted a message that incorporated the well-known Old Testament

> **1978 National Collegiate Basketball Championship**
> **PARTICIPANT PASS**
>
> **MIDEAST REGION CHAMPION**
> Sec____ Row____ Seat____
> **Session II**
> **Monday, March 27, 1978**

UK student manager Mike Murphy saved his participant pass from the title game in St. Louis. (Courtesy of Mike Murphy.)

story about David and Goliath, which he relayed late that afternoon after the team finished eating their pregame meal. He titled it "St. Louis and Five Smooth Stones," in reference to the five stones with which David armed himself to duel with Goliath.[1]

"I mention these two not to imply, you understand, that in tonight's contest Kentucky is a David and Duke is a Goliath—far from it!" Blondell told the players.

> But we all know that the biblical battle was a real test. With that being said, let me say, therefore, tonight's battle is also a real test. And to no one's surprise it's for *THE* prize in NCAA basketball. . . .
>
> Like David, your task tonight—so to speak—is to slay your opponent: that is, you've come to this point, which is not simply the climax of this season but, for some, to the zenith of your young career. And you're here to take home the trophy. . . .
>
> Make no mistake about it, those five guys on the Duke team are also confident they will be victorious. And like them, you've subdued other good and talented teams in order to get here for this contest. And as you know, there can be only one

winner in this battle. Only you can make the Kentucky Wildcats victorious over the Duke Blue Devils and take home that trophy. Whatever the margin of victory, it takes only one decisive shot to do the job.

Then he rallied the players to "reach into that team pouch and, hurling that ball into the air, be accurate. Be deliberate. Be sure. And using the smoothness of five stones at a time (players, of course), then go slay that giant opponent!"

From 1946 to 1981, the teams eliminated during the NCAA Men's Basketball Semifinals played each other in a consolation game. That evening's consolation matchup between Notre Dame and Arkansas was decided on a last-second shot by Razorback Ron Brewer. By that time, the sense of anticipation in Kentucky's locker room was peaking. "We were getting dressed and getting taped, but it was like a bunch of lions wanting to get out of a cage," Tim Stephens said. "We couldn't wait to get out there. Our managers would come into the locker room every few minutes and tell us how much time there was left on the clock. It seemed like it was an eternity."

Chuck Aleksinas characterized the pregame mood as relaxed, which ran counter to what he had grown accustomed to. "There was no tension," he said. "It was a calm, very loose atmosphere before the last game. It hadn't been for the first thirty-one games. It was weird, really strange. Maybe a lot of players were relieved to know that the stress and expectations to win [the championship] or be a failure [in our quest] would be over. I'm not really sure."

If Coach Hall sensed tension, he chose to deflect it in an unusual way. As he reviewed the game plan with his team, he stepped inside a metal trash can, squatted down, and kept on talking. "It kind of broke everybody up," Stephens said. "He did that to take the edge off." "We thought he lost his mind," Macy added. "He was trying to demonstrate not to get sidetracked by all the distractions going on

Rick Robey, left, and Duke's Mike Gminski battle for the opening tip in the 1978 NCAA Championship game. (Courtesy of the *Lexington Herald-Leader.* Photo by Frank Anderson.)

at the Final Four. We're here to win a game and win the championship." According to Coach Hamilton, Coach Hall's display of silliness included turning his tie sideways, sticking his tongue out, and crossing his eyes. "Everybody started laughing, and he said, 'Let's go win this championship,'" Hamilton said. "It kind of broke the tension in the room, because nobody had ever seen him do that before. I thought it was a very genius, perceptive move on his part."

Coach Hall then wrote the number "40" on the green locker-room chalkboard and reflected on the task at hand. "To get the glory, we have to play forty more minutes," he told his team. "We were ready. We were mentally ready. We were physically in better shape than anybody we ever played against. We lifted all winter. And in our practices we stressed conditioning." James Lee also remembered Coach Hall writing the word "Duke" on the chalkboard. "He then drew a slash through the d and the e [and asked,] 'What does that mean?'" Lee said, referring to the letters "uk," which remained unmarred. "He said, 'This is our championship. Let's go out and get it.'" For all of Coach Hall's toughness and being perceived as stern, "he had a great sensibility about big moments and how to manage the big moment," Bolton said. "He was always good at reminding them who they were and how good they are. But he also had a great way of being relaxed and assumptive about the outcome."

As the players took to the Checkerdome floor for warm-ups, Scott Courts reflected on the past few days of his young life, having flown in from Colorado that day after his dad's passing. "I think they could smoke in the arena in those days," he said. "I remember a haze in there. I remember how high I jumped in the warm-ups, and I looked through the portals, and I remember talking to my dad in my heart, saying, 'Man. We made it.'"

A capacity crowd gathered in the Checkerdome for the final game of the 1977–1978 NCAA Division I Men's Basketball season: number-one-ranked Kentucky, with a record of 29–2, versus number-eight-ranked Duke, with a record of 27–6. NBC broadcast the matchup. A fan's sign that hung over one of the Checkerdome's exits read, "If you lead a good life, say your prayers and go to church, when you die you will go to Kentucky." Another read, "Duke is no fluke." Dick Enberg handled play-by-play duties, with analysis from Al McGuire, Billy Packer, and Curt Gowdy.

Prior to tip-off, Bill Keightley informed Coach Parsons that the team was short one sideline chair, so Parsons took up the issue with an NCAA official nearby. "Read your rule book," the official told him. "I said, 'Well, Arkansas had twenty-two cheerleaders. How many are they supposed to have?' He said, 'OK. You can have your chair.' They just didn't like us. It was that simple. They thought we were too physical. Before the game, an official said to us, 'We're going to call it close.'" That's the only time Coach Parsons remembered hearing such a comment during his ten-year tenure as UK's assistant coach for men's basketball.

In addition to the "fun versus no fun" comparisons, the matchup between Kentucky and Duke was billed as experience versus youth. Kentucky had three seniors in the starting lineup: Givens, Robey, and Phillips, followed by Claytor and Macy. Duke started freshman Gene "Tinkerbell" Banks, freshman Kenny Dennard, sophomore Mike Gminski, sophomore John Harrell, and junior Jim Spanarkel. Kentucky enjoyed depth at every position, while Duke's bench was thin by comparison. However, the Blue Devils were formidable opponents known for their intelligent play and strong transition game. They also led the nation in free-throw shooting, and their coach, Bill Foster, shared the NCAA's 1977–1978 "Coach of the Year" honors with Abe Lemons of the University of Texas.

As players from both teams approached center court for the tip-off, "you could feel the tension in the air," Robey said. "It was a tense moment for us all. Each player kind of goes through his own rituals before a ball game. But once that ball's thrown up, whatever

The Wildcats work to get a stop on defense against the Blue Devils. (Courtesy of the *Lexington Herald-Leader*. Photo by Frank Anderson.)

nerves you had are gone. You're out there doing what you need to do." The Wildcats won the opening tip, but Duke's Gminski scored the game's first points, which came from free throws he made after a foul by Phillips. On the next possession, Robey scored Kentucky's first points by taking Gminski one-on-one in the paint. Phillips put UK up for the first time, 4–2, on free throws, after drawing a foul by Duke's Banks, who earned honors that season as the 1977–1978 Atlantic Coast Conference Rookie of the Year.

While watching a replay of the semifinals game between Notre Dame and Duke two nights earlier, Kentucky's coaches and players noticed how the Blue Devils left the middle open in their 2–3 zone. The Wildcats exposed that soft spot and fed Givens, a strategy that worked to perfection. "They had to extend out to play the guards, so that left the zone area where I got most of my shots from 15 to 17 feet open," said Givens, who scored 23 points in the first twenty minutes of play, including 16 straight to close out the half. "I was able to get shots, and they never made an adjustment to take those

Jack Givens (21) puts up a shot against Duke's Kenny Dennard (33) while Mike Gminski (43) looks on. (Courtesy of UK Athletics.)

shots away, so it played into my hands. I just kept shooting the ball, and the guys kept getting it to me, so it was good."

"Some of his shots were like lasers," LaVon Williams remarked. "That was an incredible performance he had that night."

Macy said it made his job as point guard "a lot easier seeing Jack get hot like that. The funny thing was that Duke never really adjusted their zone. They had the middle section open, so we'd flash Jack in there, and we tried to drop him a pass. If he got it, Gminski would either be slow to come up and he'd shoot a shot, and if he didn't come up to try and block the shot and shoot and miss, [Jack] was quick enough; he'd go around him and tip it back in. They never made a change. I don't know if they didn't feel like they could guard us man-to-man or whatever."

Banks tied the game at 22 with more than eight and a half minutes left in the first half, but UK regained the lead and returned to the locker room at halftime up by a score of 45 to 38. True to Duke's proficiency at the charity stripe, 12 of their first 20 points were free throws, and they finished the first half by sinking 20 of 21 free-throw attempts. When Hall reached the locker room, he walked to the blackboard, crossed out the number "40," and wrote "20."

About two minutes into the second half of play, NBC's Dick Enberg announced that someone had telephoned the Checkerdome and threatened the life of Gene Banks. "The police are aware of it," Enberg told viewers as Banks readied himself on the free-throw line after being fouled by James Lee in the paint. "The security is very heavy. The coach of Duke knows. It's important that this becomes a part of tonight's story. Gene Banks does not know."

"That's really a sick situation for a beautiful thing here like the NCAA Championship," Al McGuire added.

The *Chicago Tribune*'s David Israel[2] reported that an operator at the Checkerdome switchboard received the call about a half hour before game time. The threat was never acted upon, and eighteen-year-old Banks wasn't informed of the situation until after the game. (After learning of the call, he said, "Maybe later, maybe I'll be scared later. Inside I may feel it, but outside I doubt I'll show it.")

UK stuck to its game plan in the second half and built a 14-point lead with fewer than fourteen minutes left in regulation after Robey pump-faked Gminski down low and stretched from one side of the lane to the other to collect his 16th point of the game. At the 12:43 mark, Givens outmaneuvered Gminski under the basket for his 31st point—a put-back shot that gave UK its largest lead of the game at 66–50.

The Blue Devils fought back and cut UK's lead to 9 points with 10:30 left, but they had no answer for Givens, who continued

Kyle Macy is defended by sophomore John Harrell of Duke. (Courtesy of the *Lexington Herald-Leader*. Photo by Frank Anderson.)

to pour on points in the second half, including a jumper from the baseline at the 3:48 mark that grazed the top corner of the backboard before falling through the basket. When Coach Hall saw that shot, "I said to myself, 'This game's over!'" he said. "He just got in a rhythm."

With two minutes left in regulation, the Wildcats led 88–78 following a stretch of scoring that included a tip-in by Williams, a one-handed dunk by Robey on a missed shot by Shidler, and a layup by Givens. At the 1:23 mark, Duke forward Kenny Dennard fouled Claytor, who connected on the first of two free-throw attempts. In a scramble for the missed second free throw, Gminski fouled Robey, who earned a trip to the charity stripe. He sank both of his free throws, which put the Cats back up by eleven, 91–80.

After Dennard fouled Macy with thirty-five seconds left, Hall sequentially inserted the reserves who had seen little or no action in the game: Casey, Courts, Cowan, Gettelfinger, and Stephens. Macy made one of two free throws to make the score 92–84 before heading to the bench.

With twenty-three seconds to play, Casey fouled Duke's sophomore guard Bob Bender, who sank both free throws to cut Kentucky's lead to six, 92–86. Hall then put Robey, Givens, Macy, Lee, and Shidler back in the game.

With twenty-one seconds left, Harrell fouled Shidler on an inbounds pass from Macy. Shidler missed the first free throw, and Duke's Gminski grabbed the rebound and quickly passed to Bender, who dribbled the ball down court. He then dished it off to Gminski, who hit a mid-range jumper with twelve seconds left to pull the Blue Devils within four points, 92–88. They'd get no closer.

James Lee scored the final basket of the game with four ticks remaining on the clock: a left-handed power dunk, fed by a two-handed pass from fellow senior Robey beyond midcourt. That made the final score 94–88. "To bring home a championship for the state was great, and to end it all with a dunk was the highlight of my career," Lee said.

Somewhere, Adolph Rupp cracked a smile. Kentucky was back on top of college basketball. After the buzzer sounded, "I was happy, but Truman Claytor was crying," Cowan said. "I looked at him and said, 'Get ahold of yourself!' Truman looked at me and said, 'You don't know what you just did.' That stuck in my mind. Now I understand what he was talking about. Since then, people always remem-

Kentucky players react from the sideline as the final seconds tick off the clock during the 1978 NCAA Championship game. (Courtesy of the *Lexington Herald-Leader*. Photo by Frank Anderson.)

ber you. Even today, people come up to me and ask, 'Did you play at UK?'" Robey described the moments after the game as "probably one of the greatest feelings in the world. Our dream finally came true. We seniors worked hard for four years and were finally able to accomplish what we went there for. It was definitely a rewarding feeling."

When Joe Dean Jr. finished congratulating his fellow coaches, the players, and the managers, he walked into the stands to hug his dad, Joe Dean Sr., an Indiana native who became a star player for the LSU Tigers and later assumed the role of LSU's athletic director. "He was a big part of my basketball life, and I knew what it meant to him for me to be part of a national championship team, so I went and found him and did that," he said. "It was an incredible experience. I remember thinking to myself, 'Gosh. This is my first year as a full-time college coach, and this coaching stuff is kind of easy.' I

James Lee collects his commemorative championship wristwatch after Kentucky's victory against Duke. He sealed the win by throwing down a left-handed dunk with four seconds left in the game. (Courtesy of the *Lexington Herald-Leader*. Photo by Frank Anderson.)

used to remind Coach Hall, 'You hadn't won the championship in twenty years until I got here. And then I get here, and we win it!'"

For his part, Coach Hall acknowledged the pressure that he

and his team felt all season long. "It's tremendous, the responsibility I feel," he said after the game.[3] "The pressure to continue what Coach Rupp started is mine. My job is a tough job. I respond by hard work. Nothing deters me."

Givens finished with 41 points on 18 field goals and 5 free throws, earning him Most Outstanding Player honors. "Givens beat us in every conceivable way," Duke coach Bill Foster told reporters that night.[4] "He made everything he threw up. I don't think anybody scored that many points on us all year. He just had a fantastic game." Givens's scoring performance marked the third best in NCAA Championship history, behind the 43 points UCLA's Bill Walton scored against Memphis State in 1973 and the 42 points UCLA's Gail Goodrich scored against Michigan in 1965. Givens finished his career with 2,038 points, which ranks him as the third all-time leading scorer in UK men's basketball history, behind Dan Issel (2,138) and Kenny Walker (2,080).

Robey ended the final game of his UK career strong as well, scoring 20 points and pulling down 11 rebounds. He currently ranks twenty-third on the list of all-time leading scorers in UK men's basketball history, with 1,395 points, and number nine on the list of career leaders in rebounds (838, for an average of 8 per game).

Phillips, who scored 4 points and grabbed 2 rebounds against Duke, currently ranks twenty-fifth on the list of all-time leading scorers in UK men's basketball history, with 1,367 points. Lee, who scored 8 points and grabbed 4 rebounds against the Blue Devils, finished his Wildcat career with 996 points.

Once the team returned to the Checkerdome locker room, Williams remembered Bill Keightley turning away people who'd sneaked in looking for a keepsake. "We had a celebration in there, and some of the alumni came in and tried to take the uniforms," Williams said. "At one point [Bill] was going around getting everybody to put everything up before it disappeared." Coach Parsons

Coach Hall and his players celebrate the victory against Duke, which marked UK's thirteenth win in a row. The Wildcats began the 1977–1978 season with a 14–0 record. (Courtesy of the *Lexington Herald-Leader*. Photo by Frank Anderson.)

recalled one of the team managers informed him that NCAA officials had come to the locker room and asked for the game ball. "At that point, we had played well enough to have the championship trophy, so the possession of the game ball wasn't that significant," Parsons said.

Posing with the 1978 NCAA Championship trophy in the Checkerdome locker room are, from back row left, Don Sullivan, Joe Dean Jr., Tripp Ramsey, and Rob Bolton. Pictured in the foreground are Walt McCombs (left) and Coach Hamilton's son, Lenny. (Courtesy of Don Sullivan.)

Coach Hamilton remembered some players shedding tears in the locker room and hearing comments from them like "It's been tough. We stuck together. We believed in each other. We played unselfishly." "When they got chastised, they didn't take things personally," Hamilton said of this team. "It was an unselfish spirit, a matured focus that represented all the things that I thought were good about college basketball."

The *Louisville Courier-Journal's* Bob Hill reported that jubilant Wildcats fans streamed out of the Checkerdome and onto the streets of St. Louis. "In a few minutes the lobby of Stouffer's hotel, the Kentucky headquarters, was under siege," he wrote.[5] "There were Wildcat rooters on, in and under furniture. The lobby was littered with bottles. The celebration took a creative turn as five tables in a bar were pushed together and covered with water. The fans then dove onto one tabletop and slid across the other four."

The night went differently for Courts, who quietly flew coach class from St. Louis to Minneapolis in order to pay last respects to his father. "It was like a strange dream," he said. "I ended up in Minnesota, and the next day I was in the funeral procession, following a green hearse carrying my father's remains and standing in the family graveyard in the little rural farming community of Jeffers, saying goodbye. I just couldn't assimilate the drama of losing my father and winning the Final Four simultaneously. All told, it was an incredible, manic experience."

10

Extraordinary Reception

Freshman student manager George L. Fletcher did not travel with the team to St. Louis, so he watched the television broadcast near UK's campus with friends. After Lee's monster dunk sealed the victory for Kentucky, revelers began to celebrate an end to the twenty-year national-title drought. "I'd never seen so many people out in the street in my life, all up and down Euclid Avenue," Fletcher said. "It was crazy. I don't remember any couch burnings or things like that like they do these days, just people out climbing poles and doing those things."

According to the *Courier-Journal*'s Bob Hill, thousands of students gathered in the Commons area of UK, where they "chanted, set off fireworks, and climbed trees."[1] Other students and fans flocked to Lexington's airport, Blue Grass Field, to greet the team when its charter plane landed. Emotions turned destructive in some cases. Hill reported that revelers damaged an X-ray security station, an elevator, and payphones, "broke display cases and littered the floor ankle-deep in beer cans and liquor bottles. People passed out, fainted, or fell asleep on top of one another. There were two holes

An airport security guard surveys the crowd of fans who packed the terminal at Blue Grass Field (Airport) in Lexington to welcome home the Wildcats after their victory against Duke in St. Louis. (Courtesy of the *Lexington Herald-Leader*. Photo by Ron Garrison.)

in the ceiling of a car rental agency where fans, looking for a better view, fell through thin plaster."

During the team's flight from St. Louis to Lexington, someone radioed the pilot to suggest disembarking at the main airport terminal instead of the private terminal as planned to appease the burgeoning crowd, which was estimated to be between seven thousand and ten thousand strong. The plane touched down at Blue Grass Field just after 3:30 a.m. "When the tires hit the blacktop, I glanced out the window, and there were people hanging from the airport fences," Tony Sosby said. "It was a sea of people in the parking lot. It almost reminded me of the celebration for The Beatles: kids jumping over things and running out toward the plane."

As the players disembarked from the plane and walked toward the terminal, "there were people hollering at us, and it was like bedlam," Tim Stephens said. Police escorted the team to an upstairs

An estimated seven thousand to ten thousand Kentucky fans crowded in and around the terminal at Blue Grass Field to greet the returning Wildcats. (Courtesy of the University of Kentucky Archives.)

balcony inside the terminal, where they passed the NCAA Championship trophy around and took in steady waves of adulation from fans huddled below. "You couldn't stir 'em with a stick; people were shoulder to shoulder everywhere," Stephens said. "I'd never seen anything like it in my life."

The sea of fans who gathered at the airport in the wee morning hours did so "because they were living our experience," Gettelfinger observed. "It's about Kentucky winning, the idea that 'we' won. It's about them, not us [players]. If it were just about us, you'd have two Kentucky fans. There are millions of Kentucky fans across the country, because it's about them. Kentucky basketball is great because of the fans—not because of all of the players that have come through. The players came through there because UK basketball has such support."

With chants of "Goose" as a backdrop inside the terminal,

Coach Hall (left) and Rick Robey marvel at the mob of fans who gathered at Blue Grass Field terminal upon the team's return to Lexington on March 28, 1978. (Courtesy of the *Lexington Herald-Leader*. Photo by Ron Garrison.)

Marla Ridenour and Gene McLean of the *Lexington Herald* reported fans holding signs that read, "Joe Hall for President" and "We Won This One for Adolph."[2] Even seventy-nine-year-old former Kentucky governor A. B. "Happy" Chandler made his way through the crowd to deliver his congratulations. "When Adolph (Rupp) won his last one, they called me down out of the stands to accept the cup," he told the reporters. "I wish I could have been there this year. I was tied up in a business arrangement. But when my boy James Lee took the ball down the left side and dunked it, I knew it was all over then. That was the last gasp for the boys from Duke."

Some of the players had left their cars in the Blue Grass Field parking lot, but amidst the celebration chaos it became clear that they'd have to come back the next day to retrieve them. A bus shuttled the team back to campus. "Truman Claytor started hollering out, 'Guys. They tell me we can't get down Versailles Road! Ver-

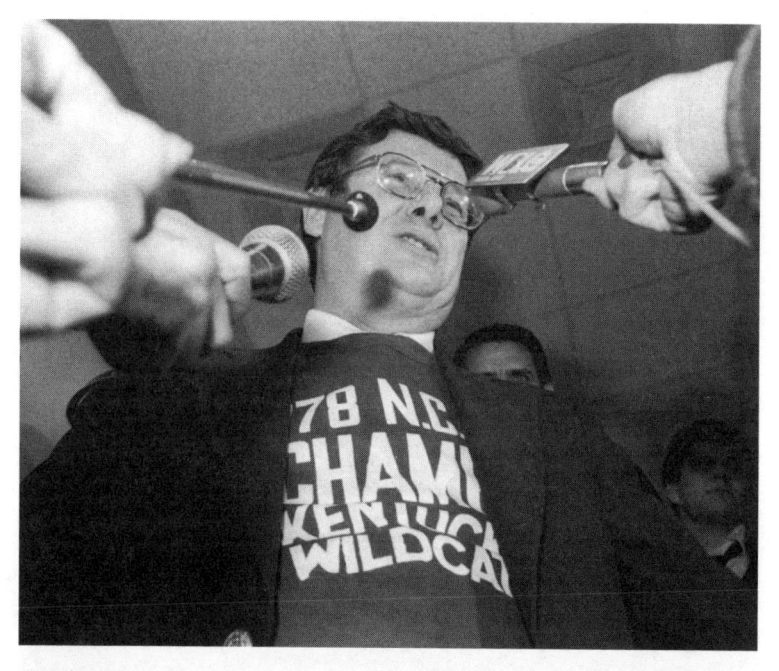

Coach Hall spoke to the media after he and the team arrived at Blue Grass Field. (Courtesy of the *Lexington Herald-Leader*. Photo by David Perry.)

sailles Road is packed! We can't get down Versailles Road!'" Dean recalled. "People were still at the airport celebrating, and we had to take a back route to the horse farms to get back to campus."

Once back in Wildcat Lodge, "I think I slept for two days," LaVon Williams said. "You don't realize how much you'd put into it. It was a great joy, but then you think about all the steps you had to go through and what you had to do to get to that point. Losing wasn't an option."

That evening at seven o'clock, an estimated fifteen thousand fans gathered for a rally in Memorial Coliseum to shower their Wildcats with praise, and seven thousand more gathered outside the arena to listen to the festivities on loudspeakers. Others watched from their home television sets. One of the dignitaries on hand,

The NCAA National Championship banner was unveiled during a special ceremony in Memorial Coliseum on March 28, 1978. (Courtesy of the *Lexington Herald-Leader*. Photo by David Perry.)

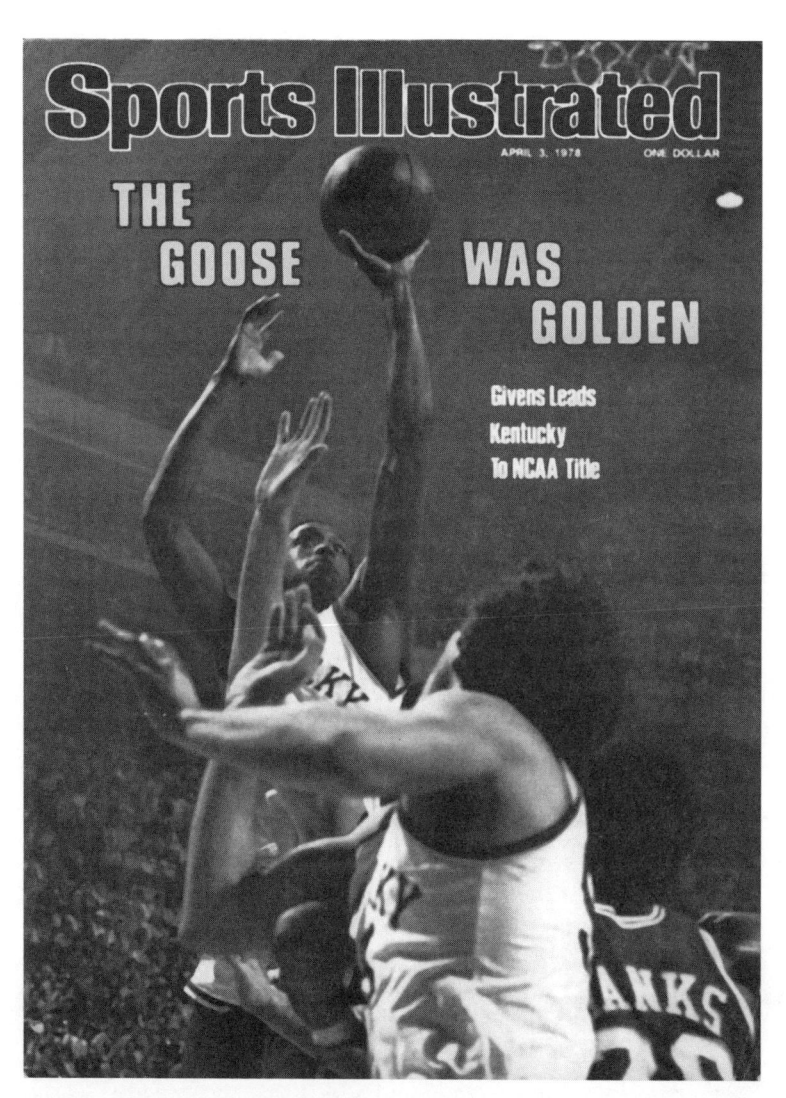

Following Jack Givens's 41-point performance against Duke, *Sports Illustrated* featured him on the cover of its April 3, 1978 issue. (Courtesy of Jack Givens.)

Governor Julian M. Carroll, proclaimed March 28 through April 4 as "Wildcat Week" in the Commonwealth of Kentucky, and Lexington mayor Jim Amato announced that the Urban County Government had adopted a resolution honoring the team's accomplishments.[3] No doubt some heads turned when Louisville mayor William Stansbury proclaimed that particular day "UK Wildcat Day in the city of Louisville." Hall addressed the crowd and said that two developments brought him nearly as much joy as winning the national title: winning "on Indiana's floor and, then, learning that it's Wildcat Day in Louisville."

Every player, coach, manager, and staff member of the team was introduced to the crowd, and a slide show of the players as children was projected on a screen set up behind the stage, to the tune of Barbra Streisand's 1973 hit "The Way We Were." Governor Carroll, Coach Hall, and Athletic Director Cliff Hagan ended the celebration by leading all who had gathered in a rendition of Stephen Foster's "My Old Kentucky Home." Weep no more, indeed.

On April 3 of the following week, Kentucky senator Wendell Ford stood before the US Senate to introduce Senate Resolution 427, a measure intended to formally commend the 1977–1978 University of Kentucky men's basketball team.[4] "The championship is particularly rewarding to the four seniors on the team: Jack Givens, Rick Robey, Mike Phillips, and James Lee," Senator Ford said during his pitch to fellow lawmakers.[5] "These young men have given four years of basketball that will long be remembered as one of the truly great eras of Kentucky basketball." He praised Coach Hall's role in the team's "impressive record" and added that the Wildcats' coach "remains strongly committed to teaching and motivating young men to succeed in the classroom as well as on the basketball floor. He has not—let me repeat not—lost sight of the fact that education is the number one priority for our institutions of higher learning. Kentucky is fortunate to have an individual of Joe Hall's ability and integrity in this position, and the future for UK's basketball program is indeed bright and promising."

Senate Resolution 427 passed by unanimous consent on the same day.

11

Beyond the Title

Every now and then, members of this team and their families gather to celebrate that special season forty years ago. "We're one of the few teams that have reunions consistently," Sullivan said. "We're still a very close-knit group that still enjoys being with each other."

Some occasions to reconvene have come unexpectedly, including memorial services for Dr. V. A. Jackson, who passed away on March 1, 1997, and Bill Keightley, who died on March 31, 2008. More recently, they gathered at a memorial service for Mike Phillips, who passed away after a fall at his home in Madisonville, Kentucky, on April 25, 2015. He was fifty-nine. On April 23 Phillips left a voice mail on Scott Courts's cell phone: "Give me a holler back, man. Just trying to talk to all the old guys I ain't talked to." Courts returned his call the next day, and they spoke for thirty minutes. "My last words to him were 'I love you, brother,' and he said the same thing to me," Courts said. "He would lose his life the next day. He had always been so invincible and larger than life. It was devastating to lose my dear brother and teammate; I'll never get over the loss."

"When we needed him—when I got in foul trouble or something—he always would step up and make it happen," Robey added.

During halftime of UK's game against Auburn on February 9, 2013, members of the 1977–1978 Wildcats were honored in Rupp Arena to mark the thirty-fifth anniversary of their championship season. (Courtesy of Victoria Graff.)

"He never complained. We were at an autograph session a few months before he died, and he said, 'It's so nice that we're all still here.' Then for that tragic accident to happen. He's going to be missed."

Every member of the team served as an honorary pallbearer. At the service, Tim Stephens said that about one month before his death, Phillips, an outdoor enthusiast, called to say he was creating knife handles out of deer and elk antlers and offered to make him one. "I decided that if I were lucky enough to kill a buck the next year that had a rack that I felt would make a good knife handle, then I was going to send it to him, and he was going to make me a knife," Stephens said. "Even though we hadn't been in each other's presence for a couple of years, he was reaching out to try to do something for me. I was appreciative of him thinking of me."

"Put me in, coach!" In April 2012, the University of Kentucky unveiled a four-hundred-pound bronze statue of Joe B. Hall outside of Wildcat Coal Lodge as a tribute to his accomplishments as the former men's basketball coach. (Photo by Doug Brunk.)

Stephens then relayed a story from his freshman year at UK. The coaching staff got word that he, Shidler, Williams, and Phillips had skipped a few academic classes, so Coach Parsons instructed them to meet him at Memorial Coliseum one Saturday at six o'clock in the morning. "He loaded us four up in a van, and he started driving out Tates Creek Road a pretty good way, and then he pulled off to the side of the road," Stephens said. He ordered everyone except Phillips to get out and to run back to Memorial Coliseum. "Evidently, Mike had missed many classes, so he took him *way* out Tates Creek Road," Stephens said. "Jay, LaVon, and I were jogging back to Memorial Coliseum and kind of joked, 'I bet Coach Parsons takes him all the way to Richmond!'"

As the trio reached the final stretch of their punishment run, they approached a small shopping complex on the edge of campus that contained a coffee shop and other merchants. When they passed by, Stephens noticed that Phillips was exiting the coffee shop with a bag of donuts. "Somehow he had managed to hitch a ride and get dropped off," Stephens said. "We were all laughing because that's the way Mike was. If there was a way to beat the system, Mike was gonna do it."

Jay Shidler said that he was closer to Phillips than to his other teammates. "He kind of took me in under his wing when I got here [and] lived next door to me in the dorm before we moved into Wildcat Lodge," Shidler said. "I didn't have a car, so I drove with Mike to every practice and to every game. We were together a lot. I felt like a little brother to him. I miss him; we lost a good one."

One day in 2013, James Lee and his fiancée were shopping in a Lexington Walmart when a woman approached Lee and said, "You don't remember me, but I want to thank you for what you did for my son."

Taken aback, Lee said, "Ma'am, help me out with this. I'd like to know what you're talking about."

She explained that during Lee's senior year, the basketball office granted a request made by her young son for Lee—his favorite Wildcat—to visit him in a Lexington hospital, where he lay terminally ill from leukemia. The family was told that Lee would visit only once, "but you kept coming back to see him," his mother said to Lee that day, with tears welling up in her eyes in the middle of a shopping aisle. "You meant so much to him, what you did."

Scores of such Wildcat goodwill stories abound, but Lee's reconnection with the past that day illustrates a larger, basic tenet of playing basketball at Kentucky: You're never forgotten. You're forever in the fold, and you can't underestimate your potential impact on others. Coach Calipari refers to Kentucky basketball players present and past as "La Familia." It's a fitting descriptor, and when you're

In April 2016, Maker's Mark issued commemorative bottles of bourbon honoring Kentucky's 1978 NCAA Men's Basketball Championship, and former Coach Joe B. Hall. Proceeds benefited UK's Center for Academic and Tutorial Services. (Photo by Z.)

part of a championship team, perhaps you're revered a little more. Anyone affiliated with the 1978 championship Wildcats will tell you that. They understand their place in Wildcat history as life moves along. "I know we've had some great teams at Kentucky," Stephens said. "I don't know if we were the greatest, but we were one of toughest teams we've ever had at Kentucky, if not the toughest—mentally and physically." Because of his knee injury, "I was never able to accomplish what I'd hoped to accomplish as an individual player," he continued. "Since I wasn't able to reach the individual accolades I'd like to have been able to, I look at the other side of the coin and think, 'Man. How many people get to be on a national-championship team?' It means more to me every year."

Dwane Casey said that members of this team not only worked hard, they shared an unwavering camaraderie. "We fought through adversity through the entire season, and we stayed together," he said. "Coach Hall made it feel almost like an 'us versus them' mentality. We could have easily lost a few more games, but the killer instinct and the togetherness we had was second to none. We won a lot of it on grit and hard work and togetherness." He added that his experience playing on a championship team at Kentucky and as an assistant coach for the 2011 NBA champion Dallas Mavericks taught him how difficult winning a national title is at any level. "When you're competing, you draw back from those times of how hard it is," said Casey, who said that he favors wearing his Kentucky NCAA Championship ring over his NBA Championship ring. "It's a journey you go through to win the championship. My saying to my players now is, 'Hard things are hard.'"

For Tripp Ramsey, serving as the graduate assistant coach for this team meant deepening a bond with his father, Frank, a native of Madisonville, Kentucky, who was a member of Kentucky's 1951 National Championship squad, which defeated Kansas State 68–58. He characterized his five years at UK as "the best time of my life,

Scores of fans camped out overnight at Keeneland in order to secure a spot in line for the April 15, 2016, Maker's Mark commemorative-bottle signing by Coach Hall and members of the 1977–1978 Wildcats basketball team. (Photo by Z.)

and it was solely because of being a part of the basketball family," Ramsey said. "I count my blessings that I was able to be a part of the family. I wasn't the player that my dad was, but I came to realize that I could still make a contribution other than playing."

Family ties to the achievement also stand out for Joe Dean Jr. His father, Joe Dean Sr., tried out for Kentucky in 1949 but ended up attending LSU, where he had a standout career and became the first Tiger to be selected in the NBA draft. Joe Dean Jr., meanwhile, was a three-year letterman for Mississippi State through the 1976–1977 season, so he had competed against Givens, Robey, Lee, and Phillips before Hall hired him to be an assistant coach in Lexington. "Growing up in a basketball family [with] basketball being kind of the center of your life, to be a part of a championship team was incredibly special," Dean said. "I'll always appreciate Coach Hall for

Catching up for breakfast in late 2015 are, from left to right, Tripp Ramsey, Don Sullivan, George L. Fletcher, and Rob Bolton. (Courtesy of Rob Bolton.)

giving me that opportunity because he could have hired one hundred different people in that position that year. He chose me for whatever reason, and I'll always be indebted to him for that."

Givens and Lee not only made citizens of their native Lexington proud, they helped pave the way for other African American athletes to wear the blue and white. Along with Casey, Claytor, Cowan, and Williams, they became the first African American basketball players to be part of a national-championship team at Kentucky, and they became the fourth and fifth African American basketball players to earn a degree from UK, behind Reggie Warford, Merion Haskins, and Larry Johnson. "For me, it was all about making a change," Lee said.

Big Blue Nation loves its Wildcats, even those who leave early or transfer, like Courts did after his freshman year (to Regis College), like Aleksinas did after his sophomore year (to the University of Connecticut), and like Stephens did after his junior year (to the University of the Cumberlands). "Coach Hall made a comment early on in the season," Courts recalled. "He said, 'Let me tell you something. I have chosen the highest quality people for this team. You will all keep in touch with each other forever. Your wives will keep in touch with their wives. Your children will keep in touch with their children.' He was right. To this day there isn't a guy on that team I wouldn't give a kidney to or die for. I mean that."

Aleksinas expressed similar sentiments about his teammates—and the fans. "I don't know that the fans knew how much we appreciated them," he said. "I've always said that if you were a player at Kentucky and walked through the Fayette Mall, and Michael Jordan was walking through the mall, they would ask you for your autograph first." He also reflected on the misconception that he transferred from Kentucky to UConn because of playing time or any number of rumors that floated about. "I transferred as a starting center, and I don't believe that's ever been done at Kentucky before

In December 2015, some team members reunited in Indianapolis to watch the NBA's Toronto Raptors take on the Indiana Pacers. From left are Rob Bolton, Jack Givens, Raptors head coach Dwane Casey, Tony Sosby, and Fred Cowan. (Courtesy of Rob Bolton.)

or since. I'm not proud of that. It was a personal decision to leave, and it was not the right decision. But when you're nineteen, twenty years old, you don't make the right decision sometimes." He went on to say that he is proud of his success playing basketball in the NBA and in Europe after college, "as the stigma of leaving a program usually means you are in over your head, and that wasn't the case. Additionally, many people think that because I'm from Connecticut and transferred to UConn from Kentucky, that I'm a UConn fan. Mike Phillips called me up and assumed I was rooting for UConn when they played UK for the NCAA Championship back in 2014. I corrected him, and we had a good laugh."

For fans who fret about when Kentucky will capture its next national basketball crown, Gettelfinger offered some reassurance. He likened Wildcats basketball to University of Alabama football,

Chris Gettelfinger (15) drives down the court during an exhibition game against South Korea in Rupp Arena on November 14, 1980. (Courtesy of the *Lexington Herald-Leader*. Photo by E. Martin Jessee.)

"because we have tradition," he said. "You cannot stop Kentucky basketball. John Wooden's [tenure at UCLA] was an era, and it ended. People remember where they were when Cliff Hagan and 'Wah Wah' Jones played. People remember Jack Givens, Antoine

Walker, Ron Mercer, and Anthony Davis. We are the epitome of basketball, a tradition that has taken [more than] one hundred years to produce, and it's going to be around for the next hundred years, win or lose. Enjoy the ride, enjoy the times you win, and don't fret about the losses."

12

A Shackle-Breaking Experience

Joe B. Hall

By the time official practices started for the 1977–1978 season, Kyle Macy could run all of our offense because he had redshirted the year before. He had also studied game films over the summer and gotten the other players to show him the plays in pick-up games. Kyle was a real catalyst and a coach on the floor. He was a guy that was totally for winning and had a good sense of tempo: when to slow down, when to push it. He got the players involved by being a feeder, getting the ball to the big men, and doing his balance of offense, too.

The seriousness of the team that year was so evident that we were called "the team without fun." It was unfair to characterize it that way, because you just can't have a team that doesn't have fun. But our guys didn't act silly over a win. They were just so conscious of being attentive and focused in practice and were disciplined off the floor. We had great leadership from guys like Rick, Kyle, and Jack. Those three were so into it to be champions. We had no issues.

When we came back to Lexington after winning the South-

Joe B. Hall, a native of Cynthiana, Kentucky, earned National Coach of the Year honors in 1978. He was inducted into the College Basketball Hall of Fame in 2012. (Courtesy of UK Athletics.)

eastern Conference Championship, there wasn't even a sign in Memorial Coliseum acknowledging what we'd done. There was no evidence that we had won anything. I called it a year without celebration, which added to that conception of being without fun. But it wasn't that; you can't have a team that doesn't have fun. The dedication was so heavy that it overshadowed their appearance. They never let up except on two occasions: our losses at Alabama and at LSU.

When we got to the Final Four in St. Louis, Duke was probably our biggest obstacle, but Arkansas had the "Three Basketeers" in Sidney Moncrief, Ron Brewer, and Marvin Delph. They also had a good center, but we played really well. We beat them, and Duke beat Notre Dame. When the Duke players went in the locker room after that win, they threw their coach in the shower and celebrated. It was wild. When we came to the dressing room after beating Arkansas, you could have heard a pin drop. After the guys got dressed, I said,

"We have a day off tomorrow. Tonight we'll get away from the home crowd that's in the hotel. We'll have dinner away from the hotel and go to a movie." Then Rick Robey asked, "Coach, did you tape the Duke–Notre Dame game?"

"Yes," I replied.

"We'd like to stay in the hotel," he said. "Can we watch the game film?"

"Sure," I said. They were so dedicated it was unbelievable.

In the championship game, Duke played a 2-3 zone. Hank Iba[1] always told me that if you use a 2-3 zone and you bring your guard out to pressure the opponent's guard, you have to bring your back line out too, so you don't create a hole in the middle. We had a play to run against the 2-3 zone. The first time we ran it, Jack was wide open, and he popped a little jump shot. We kept running the play for different people, but Jack was so good at that little left-hand jumper that pretty soon we overbalanced and ran him in the middle. Duke was concerned about Kyle and Truman shooting from outside and about Rick and Mike down low, so they dropped their big men and brought up their guards. As soon as I saw that, we quit running other options and kept flashing to the middle. In the second half, Jack put up a shot that skipped off the corner of the backboard and went in. I said to myself, "This game's over!" He just got in a rhythm.

I made sure everyone on the team got a chance to play in the championship game, even if it was for less than one minute, because when I played for Coach Rupp, he would not play subs. That stuck with me, so near the end of the game I emptied the bench. The significance of that win was the preparation and the dedication of the kids. They worked hard in the running program, the weight lifting, all the way through the rough practices and preparation for each opponent.

Since that time we've had a few team reunions. They've had fun reliving that experience, and they all are proud of what they accomplished. I think it changed their lives. I think it taught something to them about dedication and hard work, that good things come from your accomplishments, not from the trivial things that happen on a day-to-day basis. Your overall accomplishments throughout life are what really make you happy. We're still having joy, and fun, and celebration. Every year at NCAA Tournament time we think about the '78 team that we were a part of. It was a lesson in life experiences, that good things come from being serious about your duties, being focused. And then you have the fun. But when you get a job assigned to you, you don't expect to make light of it. You do your job, and then you have fun.

Winning the 1978 NCAA National Championship was a shackle-breaking experience for me. After the loss to UCLA in the 1975 NCAA National Championship game, I walked into the locker room, and my son, Steve, was sitting on the taping table outside the shower area. He was downhearted, hurt. He was little then, maybe twelve. I consoled him. I said, "We'll have another chance; we'll get one." So when we won in '78, that's the first thing I thought of. Steve was sitting in the Checkerdome stands with my wife and daughters. I went over and hugged him and said, "*Now* you can celebrate. I told you we'd get one." I was so moved by how that first loss hurt him. That was my celebration, going to my family. It was a "we" thing, and we got it done.

13

The Art of Being Prepared

Rob Bolton

The Checkerdome in St. Louis was a very inauspicious place to play the Final Four in 1978. When you measure it against where teams play now for the NCAA National Championship, it's night and day. It held no superior meaning as a basketball venue. It was a hockey rink, really.

We were all in the locker room after winning the national championship, and in the euphoria Coach Hall calmed everybody down. He said, "At your age right now, while you're enjoying this, I will tell you that this memory here, what you've done, will only get better with each passing year." He was 100 percent correct about that. With each passing year it gets richer and more fulfilling than it was when we were young and our lives were in front of us. When I look back on it, that championship was not just another day. It was not just another year. It was exceedingly special. What those guys accomplished is hard to do. For them to do it like a front-running racehorse, to go out there and say, "We're the best, so we're just going

After serving as a statistician during the 1976–1977 UK men's basketball season, Rob Bolton was a student manager for the next two seasons. He was also house manager at Wildcat Lodge during the 1978–1979 campaign. (Courtesy of Rob Bolton.)

to get on the floor and lead; you gotta catch us," was impressive to watch from where we were at the end of the bench.

Given my close proximity in age, I played high school basketball the same time that James Lee and Jack Givens did. I was playing in Louisville, and they were playing in Lexington, but I certainly knew who they were. I attended a state tournament and saw Jack play. I had also watched Rick Robey and Mike Phillips play as freshmen against the likes of Indiana University, and how they grew up and were solid, tough, and physical. More ingredients needed to come together to complete the 1977–1978 Wildcats. Kyle brought intangibles that held the team together well, made them quite formidable, but every player on that team that year had a part in making it special.

Adults typically were the ones casting the aspersion that this was a team that had no fun, a team that was always frowning or down-in-the-mouth looking. But this was a team of eighteen- to twenty-two-year-olds, so whatever was going on while adults may have looked at it corporately, these are guys that were having a whole lot of fun, because they were college kids. So pranks, fun, and girls, and all the things that go with being a college guy went on. How could people think they didn't? The thing that made them focused was that they were very much on a mission, because it was a team and personal goal to win the national championship. How do you ask anybody who has a goal in life that requires their attention and focus not to be focused and attentive? How many people do you know in life that have been successful who do nothing but work twenty-four hours a day, seven days a week? Successful CEOs go on vacation. Successful CEOs have hobbies and do things away from those moments. But when they're in those moments, they're focused and they're serious-minded about it. Were the guys on this team serious-minded? Heck yeah, they were. But when the curtain closed and they were off the clock, fun happened. Things like card games in the basement of Wildcat Lodge were played. Music was played loud in the dormitory. There were favorite songs, and pranks went on.

We tried to be the number-one-ranked student manager group in the country because we felt a responsibility. As managers we took pride in being totally prepared each day for practice. We knew preparation minutes for the players and coaches were valuable. Losing time between drills because we weren't thinking ahead on the schedule was something we did not want to happen. Over the course of a season, those lost minutes add up and could make a difference in game preparation. It is a little thing in the grand scheme, but in a real way we all believed we contributed. We knew some days we would be "the dog that would get kicked" when Coach Hall needed to vent about something. We might get yelled at for not moving a chair from here to there. It would seem so ridiculous, but if you thought it through you recognized what he was doing. It's hard at age eighteen, nineteen, twenty, and twenty-one to do that, just as it is hard for a player to accept criticism when it feels unwarranted. There were days Coach Hall knew "I can't criticize that player right now, but I'm going to explode if I don't criticize something." So sometimes the managers got called up and got chewed out. We had to learn to accept criticism and shrink back into seeming obscurity.

We had a disciplined, organized warm-up routine that the team went through before every game. It wasn't the same as it is today. Players didn't come out two hours before tip-off and shoot around in their sweats. It's very NBA-like now. Back then, you arrived at the arena, went into the locker room and dressed, and you sat there until twenty minutes before tip-off. You came out to the court as a team and warmed up, and you went back into the locker room with about five minutes to go before tip-off, got your final instructions, and returned to the court.

We all had our rituals. I stood under the basket during warm-ups. When the players transitioned from their organized drills to free shooting, I had a routine where I always threw a basketball to Kyle and took his warm-up. If for some reason I didn't, I worried the entire ball game. It was one of those superstitious things that I got his warm-up and I got him a ball to shoot immediately.

Another interesting thing about this team is that there was no shot clock and no three-point line, but they averaged 84 points a game, shot 54 percent from the floor, and made 76 percent of their free throws. These are statistics that you don't see today at the college level. In my mind, this team could transcend eras and play because they could do those things well.

14

A Lesson in the Value of Hard Work

Mike Murphy

I grew up in Lexington and had sold Cokes at the old Stoll Field and then Commonwealth Stadium and Memorial Coliseum from the time I was about eight or nine years old. I got to meet longtime equipment manager Bill Keightley and assistant coach Dickie Parsons while I was waiting for the games to begin at Memorial Coliseum. When I got out of high school, I met with them to ask about becoming one of the student managers for the basketball team. They wanted somebody who had a solid academic record and could keep up with the pace, because you commit a lot of time to it every day. The duties of a student manager begin when school starts and end whenever the season's over.

The 1977–1978 team was as focused as any unit in the history of Kentucky basketball, in my opinion, and of any organized sport I've ever been a part of. From the first day of practice, the focus was intense. These guys on the team had an excellent understanding of the legacy and the passion of Kentucky basketball. Everybody on the team understood how much Kentucky basketball meant to every fan in the state. Back in those days, we used to play the Blue and White scrimmages around the state before the season began. We'd go to places like Pikeville and Morehead. We'd play in high school gyms, and the people would be waiting on overpasses, in city streets, and filling the gyms. The adoration was amazing, and the fans bleed blue. This team wasn't a bunch of outcasts from all over. They committed themselves to winning that national championship not just for themselves, but for the fans of Kentucky basketball and the people of the Commonwealth of Kentucky.

During the 1977–1978 season, I spent a lot of time with Jay Shidler and Mike Phillips. Losing Mike in 2015 was sad for all of us. I still have texts from him on my phone that I can't erase. One of our last text exchanges took place on Valentine's Day of 2015, when the Wildcats team under Coach John Calipari was 25–0. We were chatting about the success of the team and how hard it is to go undefeated, especially with a bunch of young players. We always ended our texts or conversations with "Love you, Brother." His text to me that day was "Go Cats! Have a great valentines day! Love You Brudda!" Everybody on the team was an honorary pallbearer, even if they couldn't make it to the funeral. That's how close the entire team was.

Longtime equipment manager Bill Keightley, who was affectionately known as "Mr. Wildcat," had a significant influence on me, since he was in charge of all the student managers. He could be strict, and he made sure that we toed the line and did what we were supposed to do. If we were supposed to be somewhere at four o'clock, we were there. He could be hard on a player one day and his best friend/grandfather the next day. That was Bill. He taught you how to respect another human being and to do what you're asked to do without any questions. Some of my fondest memories

Mike Murphy (right) and his son, Zach (far left), pose with Bill Keightley during the 1977–1978 team's thirtieth reunion in February 2008. Both Murphys worked as basketball student managers for UK under Keightley. (Courtesy of Zach Murphy.)

are of talking to him in his office before or after practice. Bill passed along the history of Kentucky basketball to everybody else. He was the historian. I might have been folding towels or getting uniforms sorted, and he'd be going off about something Coach Rupp, Wallace "Wah Wah" Jones, Frank Ramsey, Cliff Hagan, or Larry Stamper had done in the past. He was the guy who connected the dots and team heritage from era to era, from team to team.

Bill knew my dad during my tenure as manager, but Dad passed away in 1981, right after I graduated from college. My own son, Zach, never knew my dad, but when Zach earned a spot as a student manager for five UK basketball teams during the Tubby Smith and Billy Gillispie eras, Bill became a grandfather figure for my son. In fact, when Bill Keightley passed, my son was one of the pallbearers. Bill always called me "Big Murph," and he called my son "Little Murph."

The games that stick out in my head from the '78 season include the Mideast Regional Finals in Dayton versus Michigan State and Magic Johnson; and, of course, the Final Four at the Checkerdome in St. Louis with Arkansas, which had the triplets (Sidney Moncrief, Ron Brewer, and Marvin Delph), in the National Semifinals; and the National Championship game versus Duke and Joe B.'s "Forty Minutes to Glory" pep talk. The other game I remember from that year was Senior Night against UNLV at Rupp Arena. Back in those days, the coach had only three time-outs, and TV time-outs were nonexistent, really. I remember every senior had a breakaway jam that rocked Rupp Arena. We were sitting on the bench, and that crowd was electric. It made the hair stand up on the back of your neck.

One of my lasting memories of the national championship at the Checkerdome was my lifelong friend, brother, and fellow Lexingtonian Jack "Goose" Givens with his UK cowboy hat on and the net around his neck. What a scene and what a memory, one that I will never forget. He and I still laugh about that night, even today. When our plane landed at Bluegrass Airport after returning from the NCAA Championship game in St. Louis, there were people standing on top of the rental car agencies on the outskirts of the airport property and lined up along Versailles Road. They were everywhere. In fact, the police created a line so we could walk through to the upstairs part of the airport itself, where we greeted the fans who were crowded onto the first level. At one point, I had the championship trophy in my hand and passed it around. There was even a crowd of people when we got back to Wildcat Lodge, and this was probably five o'clock in the morning. It was like being in The Beatles, something you could never have dreamed of experiencing in your life.

Being a part of this national-championship team taught me the value of hard work. Joe B. taught us how to bring people together for a common goal and combine that with relentless work and focus. That's what I do today; I'm a chief marketing officer for a major US corporation. It's all about bringing people together for a common goal and keeping the goal in sight at all times. That's how a corporation wins. That might sound like bull, but it's true. And I thank Joe B. for teaching me that.

15

A Storybook Ending

Jack Givens

From the very beginning of practice that season, I knew then we had a very good team, that we had a chance to win it all. We had a special mix of players. The other seniors and I had learned enough from previous years about how we had to work hard, but the preseason training and the practice sessions were when we really established how we were going to play. By the time the season started and we started playing real games, we knew that the hardest days for us would be in practice, because competition was fierce. We really went at one another hard in practice, so games against opponents were kind of like a vacation.

There was a perception that our team didn't have any fun, that we were too serious-minded. What's interesting is that the real heat for the businesslike approach to things fell on the coaches, when in fact it was mostly us players who set the tone, attitude, and approach that we were going to have that year. We players generated the work ethic. Of course, Coach Hall and the rest of the staff laid that out, but we had heard all of that before. It was the players that set the expectation in that first team meeting, where nothing short of a championship was going to be accepted. We were the ones who went in and had to grind it out every day going against one another. We had to step beyond what we had done before when it came to how physical, focused, and determined we were going to be. Coach Hall was criticized for how hard our training program was: the weight lifting, the extra running, and all the stuff we did. But the fact of the matter is that we players set the tone. If we ever got sent home from practice it was because we were working too hard and Coach Hall just felt that we didn't need to work anymore.

We lost at Alabama and at LSU that season, but I don't know that it was because we weren't working hard. The road games got a little tougher. The more games you win, the more focused the team you play is going to be and the more they're going to want to beat you. There probably were a couple of times we didn't match the intensity we were capable of and didn't play quite as well as we did at other times. I still don't know if that was a lack of effort. Most teams go through a stretch when they're not playing quite as well. There might have been some pressure building, too. When we got to the point when we had won fourteen or fifteen games, pressure came, but we were able to correct it quickly, which a lot of teams may not have been able to do. It's also important to note that there were some really good teams in the Southeastern Conference at that time. Fortunately, we lost to only two of them.

I've tried to relive that time just before we tipped off against the Duke Blue Devils for the NCAA National Championship game. I don't know that I prepared any differently from what I did for any other game. I know I was confident that we had the better team; that was the main thing I remember. Once I started to make shots, that confidence kept growing. I felt good. That was one of the good things about our team: if a player was having a good night, we made

Jack Givens celebrates after pouring in 41 points against Duke. As for the headwear, "someone put the hat on my head, and I just kept it," he said. (Courtesy of the *Lexington Herald-Leader*. Photo by Frank Anderson.)

sure we ran plays to get that person shots. The real key is not so much what we were doing as a team, but it was what Duke didn't do. They never made any adjustments to their zone defense. They were concerned with Rick Robey, Mike Phillips, and James Lee around the basket. We also had guys who could shoot the basketball from the outside: Kyle Macy, Truman Claytor, and Jay Shidler. Duke had to extend out to play our guards, so that left the zone area open, and I got most of my shots from fifteen to seventeen feet. They never made an adjustment to take those shots away, so it played into my hands. I just kept shooting the ball, and the guys kept getting it to me, so it was good. When that final horn sounded, it was the first time I could really relax, even for as well as I was playing and as confident as I was. We had been through a lot that year. We could finally exhale and say, "We got it done." It was a great feeling. It was wonderful to have that over with.

When we arrived back in Lexington from St. Louis, we were greeted by thousands of people at the airport. It was just chaos. People were parked from the airport all the way back to downtown Lexington, which is probably five miles. It seemed that people had walked a couple of miles just to be there to welcome us back. It was an amazing reception.

Winning a national championship created a lifelong bond for everybody who was a part of this team, and we're still extremely close. We would have been close anyway because we all liked one another, but winning the championship takes you to another level. It's been fun over forty years to live that kind of relationship with the rest of the guys on our team.

One of the best things about having participated on this ball club is being from Lexington, Kentucky. The fans considered me and James Lee as "their guys" because we were both born in Lexington and played high school basketball there. That is very important for the fans, to be a part of that and to share in that. Nowadays, fans say things like, "We haven't had a Lexington guy play at UK and be successful since maybe Dirk Minniefield, but you and James were really special." I couldn't have asked for any better place to play or better career than what I had, especially being able to end it all with a national championship.

Acknowledgments

I owe a busload of thanks to many special people who helped make this book happen. First, thanks to former University Press of Kentucky (UPK) acquisitions editor Ashley Runyon for shepherding this project through the approval process, and later to UPK's Patrick O'Dowd and his colleagues for assisting me every step of the way.

This book would not have been possible without cooperation from the former players, coaches, student managers, and other people close to the 1977–1978 Kentucky Wildcats who agreed to share memories and stories from four decades ago, some of which involved weighty life topics. I'm grateful for their kindness and their candor and humbled by their willingness to participate. Early on, the team's cocaptain, Jack "Goose" Givens, provided me with contact information for nearly every person I interviewed. He also sent out a group e-mail informing them about my efforts to spotlight this team, a gesture that became a key "assist" in launching this book. Thanks, Jack.

I owe a tip of the hat to Larry Vaught, a seven-time winner of the Kentucky Sportswriter of the Year award, and to Tom Leach, the "Voice of the Wildcats," for penning the forewords. Larry covered this team from the sidelines as a young reporter, and Tom's knowledge of Kentucky basketball history is off the charts. I'm also indebted to the following people who read early versions of this book and provided valuable feedback: Rob Bolton, Kevin Cook, Jack Givens, Coach Joe B. Hall (who also kindly gave his blessing for me to title the book after his "Forty Minutes to Glory" catchphrase), James Lee, and Kyle Macy.

The opportunity to include so much original source material for this book has been a privilege. Thanks to Coach Hall, Rob Bolton, Mike Murphy, and Jack Givens for contributing first-person essays about this special team, to Rev. David N. Blondell for unearthing the devotional he shared with the team prior to the championship against Duke, and to Dr. Roy Holsclaw and his wife, Katharine, for sharing the Wildcat Slush recipe.

Matt Harris, former research and reference coordinator at UK's Special Collections and Research Center, and Jason Flahardy, photographic archivist at the University of Kentucky Archives, were instrumental in helping me locate images and other material for this project. So was Ron Garrison, photo director at the *Lexington Herald-Leader*. For assistance obtaining other photographs I'm grateful to Rob Bolton, Dan Burgess, Kevin Cook, George L. Fletcher, Victoria Graff, Marie Jackson, Eric Lindsey, Enzina Mastrippolito, Nancy McIlvaney, Whitney Miller, Mike Murphy, Zach Murphy, Dick Parsons, and Don Sullivan. Special thanks to Mariam Addarrat at the Lexington Public Library for supplying many newspaper articles for background, and to George L. Fletcher for loaning me a book of press clippings from the 1977–1978 season to comb through, as well as a bound collection of *The Cats' Pause* newspapers from that campaign. Props as well to Wil Weston, head of collections at San Diego State University's library, for his assistance in locating a copy of Senate Resolution 427, and to Sakeenah Lambert, for facilitating my interview with Leonard Hamilton. Thanks also to Anthony Chiffolo for his assistance with copyediting.

Writing a book is like running a marathon, and I'm fortunate that so many people encouraged me from start to finish, including my parents, Bill and Genevieve Brunk, my brother, Bob, and my many far-flung relatives. Thanks as well to Dean and Ruth Cook, Kevin Cook, Matt Farmelant, Scott Farmelant, Keith Finley, Pernell and Tracey Francis, Barbara Goran, Greg Horn, Debra Isaacs, Rick and Lisa Lofgren, Wayne and Alice Rogers, Scott Rudolph, Colleen Rush, Tom Simpson, Guy Smith, and Dave Weiner. My deepest appreciation goes to my wife, Vickie, who continues to cheer me on through every mile of this "marathon" and always respects my passion for Big Blue hoops.

The 1978 NCAA National Champion Kentucky Wildcats not only hold a special place in UK basketball history, they're ingrained in my personal story as a boy who grew up in Wilmore, Kentucky. If you formed a line of kids in the Bluegrass State who counted these players as heroes in 1978, it would have stretched from Pikeville to Paducah. What young fan didn't marvel at Kyle Macy's free-throw routine and accuracy, emulate Rick Robey's hook shot, leap up from the couch in joy after witnessing one of James Lee's monster dunks on TV, and talk about the Wildcats during school lunch and recess? As I grew older, I realized that fans of all ages felt this way. Kentucky basketball brings citizens of the Commonwealth together unlike anything else. It's the great equalizer.

One Friday evening not long after UK had won the 1978 NCAA Championship, my mom and I walked into Fayette Mall in Lexington to discover Rick Robey signing autographs at a retail store. I had nothing for him to sign, but mom dug through her purse and pulled out a small blank notepad to use. I approached, shook Robey's hand, and he signed his name carefully with a black Sharpie. A few years later, I somehow made the cut on my freshman high school basketball team in a suburb of Rochester, New York. When it became apparent I'd be a forward-center, I insisted on wearing jersey number 53 that season as a nod to Robey. I remember his work ethic as being second to none, so I figured that if he could be successful with determination, grit, and discipline—all traits that defined this team—maybe there was hope for me as an adolescent trying to find his way. Forty years later, that hunch still drives me, thanks to Kentucky basketball.

Appendix 1

St. Louis and Five Smooth Stones

Rev. David N. Blondell

Note: During interviews with Rev. David N. Blondell, who had also served as senior minister of Crestwood Christian Church in Lexington, he told me that he had a hunch that he had kept notes from the devotional he imparted to the Wildcats at the end of the pregame meal in St. Louis before they battled Duke for the national championship. After searching through files at home, he unearthed key notes from that day. Published here is the devotional in its entirety.

For a few minutes I'd like to talk about an Old Testament story very familiar to us all. It's the one about David and Goliath. The whole thing is too long and detailed for my purpose here tonight—but we all know the outcome: that is, the underdog boy slays the enemy giant!

I mention these two not to imply, you understand, that in tonight's contest Kentucky is a David and Duke is a Goliath—far from it! But we all know that the biblical battle was a real test. With that being said, let me say, therefore, tonight's battle is also a real test. And to no one's surprise it's for *THE* prize in NCAA basketball.

In the biblical story, you remember, David made the decision to fight this Israelite enemy. The Philistine Goliath had insulted both the Israelites and their God, and insisted that someone come out and fight him. David, armed with only five stones from a creek, approached Goliath. They exchanged heated words, and finally the champion of the Philistines began to approach David. The shepherd boy took out a single stone from his pouch—what we would call a slingshot—and hurled it at the giant, hitting him in the forehead; and he fell dead.

What impresses me is the young boy prepared himself with five stones but used only one to complete his task and achieve his goal. Understand, he had equipped himself with the necessary ammunition. He knew his capabilities, and he trusted his faith in himself and his God to fulfill his desired goal.

All else aside, let me suggest that you will put on the floor tonight five players (at a time). Like David, your task tonight—so to speak—is to slay your opponent: that is, you've come to this point, which is not simply the climax of this season but, for some, to the zenith of your young career. And you're here to take home the trophy.

1. You're well prepared. Your coaches have perfected your game and equipped you mentally and physically.
2. You have the necessary equipment—that is, you have the talent and ability.
3. Your army here in St. Louis will back you up, cheering you on—because they believe you will do the job.
4. You have faced battles all year and are now ready for the final conquest against a revered opponent.

5. And I don't have to tell you, this time it's for all the marbles (or stones, if you prefer)!

Make no mistake about it, those five guys on the Duke team are also confident they will be victorious. And like them, you've subdued other good and talented teams in order to get here for this contest. And as you know, there can be only one winner in this battle. Only you can make the Kentucky Wildcats victorious over the Duke Blue Devils and take home that trophy. Whatever the margin of victory, it takes only one decisive shot to do the job.

So, reach into that team pouch and, hurling that ball into the air, be accurate. Be deliberate. Be sure. And using the smoothness of five stones at a time (players, of course), then go slay that giant opponent!

Appendix 2

Senate Resolution 427: A Commendation for the Wildcats

Note: On April 3, 1978, Kentucky senator Wendell Ford introduced to his colleagues in the US Senate a resolution intended to commend the University of Kentucky basketball team on winning the 1978 NCAA Men's Basketball Championship.[1] The transcript of his pitch and the resolution appear below. The transcript includes comments from two former US senators: Paul Sarbanes of Maryland and Frank Church of Idaho. A third senator, Walter Darlington Huddleston of Kentucky, is mentioned in passing.

Mr. FORD. Mr. President, as in legislative session, I send to the desk a resolution commending the University of Kentucky for winning the NCAA basketball championship and ask for its immediate consideration.

The PRESIDING OFFICER. The resolution will be stated by title. The assistant legislative clerk read as follows: A RESOLUTION

(S. RES. 427) TO COMMEND THE UNIVERSITY OF KENTUCKY BASKETBALL TEAM.

The PRESIDING OFFICER: Is there objection to the present consideration of the resolution?

There being no objection, the Senate proceeded to consider the resolution.

Mr. FORD. Mr. President, 1 week ago today the University of Kentucky's basketball team culminated a brilliant season by defeating Duke University 94–88 in St. Louis for the National Collegiate Athletic Association basketball championship. The victory enabled the Wildcats to finish the season with a 30–2 record—a feat made even more remarkable by the fact that they were ranked at the top of all the polls for the season's duration.

The championship is particularly rewarding to the four seniors on the squad: Jack Givens, Rick Robey, Mike Phillips, and James Lee. These young men have given 4 years of basketball that will long be remembered as one of the truly great eras of Kentucky basketball history.

As freshmen, they were on a team that finished second to UCLA in the 1975 NCAA final. As sophomores, they led UK to the National Invitational Tournament championship at Madison Square Garden. Last year, they were a finalist in the eastern region.

That is why it was so satisfying to see this group of seniors complete their careers with this crowning achievement. It should also be noted that during the past four seasons, Kentucky won the Southeastern Conference championship three times.

Without a doubt, the man most responsible for this impressive record is Coach Joe B. Hall, who took over as the school's head basketball coach 4 years ago. Not only has he brought the NCAA championship back to Lexington for the first time since 1958, but he remains strongly committed to teaching and motivating young men to succeed in the classroom as well as [on] the

Senate Resolution 427: A Commendation for the Wildcats

basketball floor. He has not—let me repeat not—lost sight of the fact that education is the number one priority for our institutions of higher learning.

Kentucky is fortunate to have an individual of Joe Hall's ability and integrity in this position, and the future for UK's basketball program is indeed bright and promising.

Recognition and messages of congratulation to Coach Hall and his team have come from all over the world. My colleague, Senator HUDDLESTON and I think the Senate, too, should be on record in saluting this impressive accomplishment and we ask unanimous consent that this resolution commending the University of Kentucky basketball team be adopted.

I thank the Chair.

Mr. SARBANES. Mr. President, will the Senator yield for a question of the Senator from Kentucky?

Mr. CHURCH. I yield for that purpose.

Mr. SARBANES. Mr. President, will the Senator from Kentucky enlighten us? I think this will be helpful to those from other States. What is the secret in Kentucky for producing championship basketball teams? We wish to take that secret home with us.

Mr. FORD. I wish to help Senators as best I can, but I do not think I want to divulge that secret.

It is similar to the situation when the distinguished senior Senator from Arkansas was talking about the game we played. He said he would see me but he would be on the other side of the field. They happen to play this game on a court, and if some of the teams would recognize that maybe it would work out all right.

Let me make one point, if I may, Mr. President, and I do not wish to get everyone off the trend of thought here, but the four seniors on this team and the coach of this team the first year were in the finals of NCAA, the next year they won the NIT, the next year they were in the quarter finals, and this year they won the NCAA championship.

I think that is a pretty good record for a school like the University of Kentucky. As we know, last year they only lost one football game. So maybe we are coming of age. Being an academic institution, the University of Kentucky is one of the top 33 research universities in the country. We are also coming of age in all sports.

I thank the Senator from Idaho and I owe him one.

The PRESIDING OFFICER. The question is on agreeing to the resolution.

The resolution (S. Res. 427) was agreed to.

The preamble was agreed to.

The resolution, with its preamble, reads as follows:

Whereas, the University of Kentucky's basketball team defeated Duke University on March 27 in St. Louis to win its fifth National Collegiate Athletic Association basketball championship;

Whereas, the senior members of this team, during their four-year varsity career, were also NCAA runners-up, National Invitational Tournament champions and three-time champions of the Southeastern Conference;

Whereas, Coach Joe Hall, his staff and his players displayed outstanding dedication, teamwork and sportsmanship throughout the course of the season in achieving collegiate basketball's highest honor;

Whereas, Coach Hall and the Wildcats have brought pride and honor to the Commonwealth which is rightly known as the basketball capital of the world;

Therefore, be it resolved that the Senate of the United States commend and congratulate the University on this outstanding accomplishment.

About the Author

Doug Brunk is an award-winning journalist who holds journalism degrees from Point Loma Nazarene University and the S. I. Newhouse School of Public Communications at Syracuse University. He has written hundreds of articles for consumer and trade publications. A native of Rochester, New York, he spent his formative years in Wilmore, Kentucky, where he became hooked on following the Kentucky Wildcats men's basketball team. Brunk is the author of *Wildcat Memories: Inside Stories from Kentucky Basketball Greats,* which was published by the University Press of Kentucky in 2014. He lives in San Diego with his wife, Vickie, and their dog, Genie.

Notes

Introduction

1. The NCAA did not use the term "Final Four" in radio and television broadcasts until later years, but the term was widely used by sports media during the 1977–1978 season.

2. The Michigan State Spartans and their star guard Earvin "Magic" Johnson defeated the Indiana State Sycamores and their star forward Larry Bird 75–64 in the NCAA Championship game on March 26, 1979, in Salt Lake City, Utah.

3. Freshmen were not eligible to play NCAA varsity basketball until the 1972–1973 season.

1. The Tone Is Set

1. John Clay, "Wooden's Last Victim Was UK," *Lexington Herald-Leader,* June 5, 2010.

2. Hacker retired from basketball broadcasting duties as the "Voice of the Wildcats" in the summer of 2001. His successor, Tom Leach, still holds the position.

3. *The Cats' Pause,* Dec. 3, 1977.

4. John McGill and Walt Johnson, *A Year at the Top: Kentucky Wildcats '77–'78* (Lexington, KY: Jim Host and Associates, 1978).

5. Rick Bailey, "Of All the Seniors, His Career Has Been the Most Tumultuous," *The Saturday Herald and Leader,* Mar. 4, 1978.

6. University of Kentucky, all rights reserved. University of Kentucky Athletics: William B. Keightley Oral History Project, Louie B. Nunn Center for Oral History, University of Kentucky Libraries.

7. Dan Hall transferred to Marshall University after his sophomore year. He passed away in 2013.

3. Farewell to Rupp

1. UK halted intrastate travel to play scrimmages in the early 1990s.

2. John A. McGill, "'Beautiful' Kentucky Belts Russia," *The Saturday Herald and Leader,* Nov. 12, 1977.

3. In September 2012, UK unveiled a bronze statue of Coach Hall outside the entrance to Wildcat Coal Lodge. It shows him seated and holding a rolled-up program in his right hand, with two empty chairs to his left.

4. Saint Christopher is considered the patron saint of travelers.

5. Mike Johnson, "Givens Is 'Knighted' as UK Wins the War," *The Lexington Leader,* Dec. 6, 1977.

6. Rick Bailey, "Cats Edge Jayhawks in a Tight One, 73–66," *The Saturday Herald and Leader,* Dec. 10, 1977.

7. Joe Kemp, "His Death Was Not Unexpected," *Kentucky Kernel,* Dec. 12, 1977.

8. Oscar Combs, "A Final Salute to Der Baron Adolph," *The Cats' Pause,* Dec. 10, 1977.

9. "Tough Cats Pay Tribute to 'Baron,'" *Sunday Herald-Leader,* "The Year of The Cats" supplement, Apr. 2, 1978.

10. Launched during UK's 1953–1954 campaign, the UK Invitational Tournament was discontinued after the 1989–1990 season.

11. Rick Bailey, "Wildcats Roll to UKIT Title, Exit Doghouse," *Lexington Herald-Leader,* Dec. 18, 1977.

12. D. G. FitzMaurice, "'Danger Zone' Fatal to Iona as Cats Romp," *The Saturday Herald and Leader,* Dec. 24, 1977.

13. Rick Bailey, "Iona Coach Glad Cats Deserve No. 1 Rating," *Lexington Herald,* Dec. 23, 1977.

14. Rick Bailey, "Kentucky Survives Moment of Truth with Final Spurt," *Sunday Herald-Leader,* Jan. 1, 1978.

4. Christening Wildcat Lodge

1. In a ruling that took effect on Aug. 1, 1979, the NCAA required UK to make certain modifications to Wildcat Lodge, including putting

two players per room, allowing for a certain number of nonplayers to reside there, and eliminating some of the lounge space.

2. Gail Green, "Wildcat Lodge Reward for UK Winners," *Sunday Herald-Leader,* July 9, 1978.

5. A Cold Snap and a Loss

1. According to the Bible, Peter (also known as Simon) was one of Jesus Christ's twelve apostles.

2. D. G. FitzMaurice, "On 'Super Saturday,' Cats Outclaw Tigers," *Sunday Herald-Leader,* Jan. 15, 1978.

3. Rick Bailey, "LSU's Higgs Not Upset by UK Fans," *Sunday Herald-Leader,* Jan. 15, 1978.

4. "Cats Hit 67.6 Percent in Win over Bulldogs," *Sunday Herald-Leader,* "The Year of the Cats" supplement, Apr. 2, 1978.

5. Al Browning, "'One of Our Biggest,' Says C. M. Newton," *Tuscaloosa News,* Jan. 24, 1978.

6. Navigating the "Pressure Cooker"

1. The Holsclaws made containers of Wildcat Slush for players to consume after every postseason game that year, including the national championship game against Duke.

2. Mike DeCourcy, "Kentucky Coach John Calipari: 'I've Got Maybe the Best Job in College Basketball,'" *Sporting News,* Mar. 5, 2012.

3. Rick Bailey, "Macy Magnificent as Wildcats Rip Gators Apart in 2nd Half," *Sunday Herald-Leader,* Feb. 5, 1978.

4. Rick Bailey, "Reserves Provide LSU a Reason to Celebrate," *Sunday Herald-Leader,* Feb. 12, 1978.

5. Paul Borden, "The Season," *The Courier-Journal,* Mar. 29, 1978.

6. D. G. FitzMaurice, "No 'Artistic Success,' but Cats Subdue Rebs," *Lexington Herald,* Feb. 14, 1978.

7. According to the Feb. 14, 1978, edition of *The Oxford Eagle,* the matchup with UK drew a crowd of 8,809 to the Rebeldome, the second largest in history behind a crowd of 9,132 that gathered to watch Pete Maravich and LSU play there in 1970.

8. Stuart Warner, "The Unflappable Goose an Easy Person for Anyone to Relate to," *The Saturday Herald and Leader,* Mar. 4, 1978.

9. D. G. FitzMaurice, "Robey Gets a Charge as Cats Edge State," *Sunday Herald-Leader,* Feb. 19, 1978.

10. D. G. FitzMaurice, "The Cats Are Back as Bama Falls, 97–84," *Lexington Herald,* Feb. 21, 1978.

11. D. G. FitzMaurice, "A Slice of Orange Cures All Ills," *Sunday Herald-Leader,* Feb. 26, 1978.

12. "A Return to the Top and an SEC Title, Too," *Sunday Herald-Leader,* "The Year of The Cats" supplement, Apr. 2, 1978.

13. Oscar Combs, "Farewell to Four Great Seniors," *The Cats' Pause,* Mar. 4, 1978.

14. "Cats Bomb Las Vegas 92–70 with Slam-Dunking Seniors," *The Cats' Pause,* Mar. 11, 1978.

15. D. G. FitzMaurice, "Macy's Shooting Carries Cats Past Vandy in Finale," *Lexington Herald,* Mar. 7, 1978.

7. Tourney Time

1. In 1994, the Marquette University Warriors changed their name to the Golden Eagles.

2. Roy Damer, "Hall's Risk Saves Kentucky's Hopes," *Chicago Tribune,* Mar. 19, 1978.

3. D. G. FitzMaurice, "Wildcats 'Bench' Florida St. in NCAA Opener," *Sunday Herald-Leader,* Mar. 12, 1978.

4. In 1997, the Miami University Redskins changed their name to the RedHawks.

5. D. G. FitzMaurice, "Phillips Muscles Wildcats into Mideast Region Finals," *Lexington Herald,* Mar. 17, 1978.

6. Roy Damer, "Purdue Refugee Is Kentucky Hero," *Chicago Tribune,* Mar. 19, 1978.

7. Rick Bailey, "Sooey! UK Will Meet Arkansas in St. Looey," *Sunday Herald-Leader,* Mar. 19, 1978.

8. University of Kentucky, all rights reserved. University of Kentucky Athletics: William B. Keightley Oral History Project, Louie B. Nunn Center for Oral History, University of Kentucky Libraries.

8. Meet Me in St. Louis

1. Originally known as St. Louis Arena, the facility changed its name to Checkerdome in 1977 after the checkerboard logo of Ralston

Purina, which owned the arena and the St. Louis Blues between 1977 and 1983.

2. After Coach Hall retired at the close of the 1984–1985 campaign, Sutton coached the Wildcats for four seasons.

3. Moncrief was a five-time NBA All-Star in a career that spanned 1979–1991. Delph was drafted by the NBA in 1978 and 1979 but never played in the league. Brewer played for six different NBA teams from 1978 to 1986.

4. Oscar Combs, "It's Hog-Rooting Time in St. Louis," *The Cats' Pause*, Mar. 25, 1978.

5. Stuart Warner, "Cats Turned Goose Loose against Arkansas," *Sunday Herald-Leader*, Mar. 26, 1978.

6. Bill Jauss, "Carefree Duke Waits for Grim Kentucky," *Chicago Tribune*, Mar. 27, 1978.

9. Forty Minutes to Glory

1. To read Reverend Blondell's devotional in its entirety, turn to page 169.

2. David Israel, "Death Threat, Loss Fail to Faze Banks," *Chicago Tribune*, Mar. 28, 1978.

3. Rick Bailey, "Lee's Slam Signals Beginning of Hugs, Hijinks, and Hysteria," *The Lexington Leader*, Mar. 28, 1978.

4. Rick Gosselin, "Hall's Hugs Show Feelings for His Team after Victory," *The Lexington Leader*, Mar. 28, 1978.

5. Bob Hill, "The Celebration," *The Courier-Journal*, Mar. 29, 1978.

10. Extraordinary Reception

1. Bob Hill, "The Celebration," *The Courier-Journal*, Mar. 29, 1978.

2. Marla Ridenour and Gene McLean, "Welcome Back, Cats! Thousands of UK Fans Squeeze into Airport to Cheer Nation's No. 1 Team," *Lexington Herald*, Mar. 29, 1978.

3. Marva York, "Fans Jam Memorial Coliseum to Honor Cats," *Lexington Herald*, Mar. 29, 1978.

4. To read Senate Resolution 427, turn to page 173.

5. "Commendation to the University of Kentucky Basketball Team," S. Res. 427, 95th Congress (1978).

12. A Shackle-Breaking Experience

1. Henry ("Hank") Iba was the head men's basketball coach at Oklahoma State University for thirty-six seasons before he retired in 1970. He coached US Olympic men's basketball teams in 1964, 1968, and 1972.

Appendix 2

1. "COMMENDATION TO THE UNIVERSITY OF KENTUCKY BASKETBALL TEAM," S. Res. 427, 95th Congress (1978).

Index

Page numbers in italics refer to illustrations.

African Americans, 20, 143
Aleksinas, Chuck, *24*, 29, 33, *48*, 50, 84, *92*, 109, 143–44
Allen, Forrest "Phog," 6, 46
Allen Fieldhouse, 44
Alumni Gym, 14, 15
Amato, Jim, 132
American Basketball Association (ABA), 102
Associated Press (AP), 5, 37, 89, 102
Auburn University, 67, 80, 136

Bailey, Rick, *94*
Banks, Gene "Tinkerbell," 112, 113, 115
Bender, Bob, 117
"Big Bertha," *21*
Big Blue Nation. *See* Wildcat fans
Bird, Larry, 2, 179n2
Birdsong, Otis, 49
Blanton, Jerry, 24
Blondell, David N., 65–67, 107–9, 169–71
Blue Devils. *See* Duke University

Blue Grass Field, xx, 125–29, *126*, *127*, *128*, 158
Bolton, Rob, 7, *32*, 59, *122*, *142*, *144*, *152*; 1977–1978 season and, 32, 35, 40–41, 68, 71, 91, 151–54; 1978 NCAA Championship and, 111, 122, 151–52
Brewer, Ron, 102, 109, 148, 158, 183n3
Brown, Dale, xiv, xvi, 67, 81
Bruins. *See* UCLA (University of California Los Angeles)
Bryant Hall, 55
Bulldogs. *See* Mississippi State University; University of Georgia

Calipari, John, xvii, 3, 77, 138, 140, 156
Carnesecca, Lou, 50
Carroll, Julian M., 132
Casey, Dwane, *24*, *27*, *51*, 57, *144*; 1977–1978 season and, 14, 24, 25, 27, 46, 51, 81–82, 140;

Casey, Dwane *(cont.)*
1978 NCAA Championship game and, 117, 143; 1978 NCAA Tournament play and, xvi, 91, 93
Catlett, Gale, *11*
Chandler, A. B. "Happy," 128
Checkerdome, *98*, 182–83n1; 1978 Final Four and, 97, 98, 102, 151; 1978 NCAA Championship game and, 7, 107, 111, 112, 115, 120, 122, 150, 158
Church, Frank, 173, 175
Claytor, Truman, *24, 27, 42, 51, 106;* 1977–1978 season, early games and, 42; 1977–1978 season, later games and, 72, 74, 84, 85, 88; 1977–1978 season and, xx, 13, 14, 24, 27, 37, 51, 63, 143; 1977 NCAA Tournament regional finals and, 2, 12; 1978 Final Four and, 98–99; 1978 NCAA Championship and, 7, 128–29; 1978 NCAA Championship game and, 112, 117, 149, 164; 1978 NCAA Tournament play and, xvi, 91, 93, 95–96
Combs, Oscar, 49, 86
Conner, Jimmy Dan, 18–19, *19*, 20
Cook, Norm, 49
Courts, Scott, *24, 45, 92*, 135, 143; 1977–1978 season and, xiv, 4, 15–16, 23, 24, 45, 60, 63, 64, 77, 92; 1978 NCAA Championship game and, 7, 111, 117, 123; father's death, 7, 97–98, 111, 123
Cowan, Fred, *24, 70*, 143, *144;* 1977–1978 season, later games and, 80, 81–82; 1977–1978 season and, xv, 24, 28–29, 70; 1978 NCAA Championship game and, 117–18; 1978 NCAA Tournament play and, xvi, 91
Crimson Tide. *See* University of Alabama

Dampier, Louie, 50
Daniels, Walter, *78*
Davis, Anthony, 146
Davis, Johnny, 49
Dean, Joe, Jr., *24, 61, 122;* 1977–1978 season and, 4, 13, 16, 24, 53, 61, 74, 79, 83, 141, 143; 1978 NCAA Championship and, 118–19, 122, 129; Wildcat Lodge and, 6, 56
Dean, Joe, Sr., 118, 141
Delph, Marvin, 102, 148, 158, 183n3
Dennard, Kenny, 112, *114*, 117
DePaul University, 89
Duke University, 89, 105, 106, 148. *See also* NCAA Championship game, 1978
Durham, Hugh, 92

Enberg, Dick, 112, 115
ESPN, 2
Etcheberry, Pat, 25–26

Farrell, Mark, *32*
Fighting Irish. *See* Notre Dame University
Fletcher, George L., 31, *32*, 71, 125, *142*
Florida State University, xvi, 34, 89–93
Flynn, Mike, 10, 18–19, *19*, 20
Ford, Phil, Jr., 37
Ford, Wendell, 132, 173–76
49ers. *See* University of North Carolina (UNC) Charlotte
Foster, Bill, 112, 120
Foster, Stephen, 132

Gaels, 48, 50
Gamecocks, 49–50
Gators, 67, 79
Gettelfinger, Chris, 3, 22, *24*, 31, 41, 117, 127, 144–45, *145*
Gillispie, Billy, 157
Givens, Jack "Goose," *5, 7, 13, 24, 86, 95, 99, 103, 114,* 132, 143, *144,* 145, 152, 161–64, *163;* 1975–1976 season and, 1, 10, 174; 1975 NCAA Championship game and, xix, 1, 9, 10, 174; 1976–1977 season and, xix, 1, 2, 12, 141, 174; 1977–1978 season, early games and, 43, 44, 50, 52; 1977–1978 season, later games and, 67, 72, 74, 79, 80, 81, 83, 84–85, 86, 88; 1977–1978 season and, xiv–xv, xvii, 19–20, 24, 33, 40, 63–64, 68, 77; 1977 NCAA Tournament regional finals and, xix, 1, 2, 12; 1978 Final Four and, 99, 103; 1978 NCAA Championship game and, xiii–xiv, xx, 107, 112, 113–14, 115–17, 120, 131, 149, 158, 162–64, 174; 1978 NCAA Tournament play and, xvi, 91, 93, 95, 96; as freshman, xix, 9, 10, 13, 18–19, 20, 174; as leader for 1977–1978 season, xix–xx, 14–15, 16, 18, 22, 86, 147, 161, 174; qualifications, 3, 5, 9, 16, 18; resolve to win, 2, 4, 5, 9, 12, 14; on the cover of *Sports Illustrated,* 131
Gminski, Mike, *110,* 112, 113, *114,* 115, 117
Golden Eagles. *See* Marquette University
Gomelsky, Alexandr, 43
Goodrich, Gail, 120
Gowdy, Curt, 112
Green, Gail, 55, 56
Grevey, Kevin, 10, 18, *19,* 20, 40
Grunfeld, Ernie, 49
Guyette, Bob, 10, 18–19, *19,* 20

Hacker, Marilyn, 77, 79
Hacker, Ralph, xiv, 4–5, 10, 18, 49, 77, 79, *94,* 105, 179n2.2
Hagan, Cliff, 132, 145, 157
Hale, Jerry, *19*
Hall, Dan, *13,* 20, 180n7
Hall, Joe B., *7, 11, 24, 30, 58, 72, 106, 121, 128, 129,* 137, 139, 141, 147–50, *148,* 180n3,

Hall, Joe B. *(cont.)*
183n2; 1975 NCAA Championship game and, 9–10, 150; 1977–1978 season, later games and, xiv, 81, 85; 1977–1978 season and, xx, 24, 75, 79, 143, 176; 1978 Final Four and, xvii, 100, 102, 105, 148–49; 1978 NCAA Championship and, xxi, 37, 119–20, 128, 129, 132, 150, 151, 174, 176; 1978 NCAA Championship game and, xiii–xiv, xix, xx, 116, 117, 121, 149, 150; 1978 NCAA Tournament play and, xvi, 89–93, 94, 96; becoming head coach, 11, 20, 34; commemorative statue of, *137;* official practices, 29, 31, 32, 33, 37–38; pre-1978 NCAA Championship game and, 105–6, 107, 109, 111, 148–49, 158; resolve to win and, 4, 13, 37; Adolph Rupp and, 11, 43, 44–46; as taskmaster, 4, 5, 14, 16, 19–20, 21, 28, 63, 67, 81–82, 153–54, 159, 161–62, 174–75; as taskmaster during games, 43–44, 53, 83, 91, 140; US Senate Resolution 427 and, 132–33, 174–75, 176; weight training and, 25, 26; Wildcat Lodge and, 6, 55, 58, 62
Hall, Steve, 150
Hamilton, Lenny, *122*
Hamilton, Leonard, 5, 10, 18, *24,* *34,* 53, 67, 80, 111, 122; 1978 NCAA Tournament play and, xvi, 94
Harrell, John, 112, *116,* 117
Haskins, Merion, 20, 143
Heathcote, Jud, 93
Higgins, Barbara, *32*
Higgs, Kenny, 67, 80
Hill, Bob, 122–23, 125–26
Holmes Hall, 55, 57, 62
Holsclaw, Katharine, 76, 181n1.2
Holsclaw, Roy, 75–76, 181n1.2
Hoosiers. *See* Indiana University
Huddleston, Walter Darlington, 173, 175

Iba, Hank, 149, 184n1
Indiana State University, 179n2
Indiana University, xix, 12, 44, 89, 102, 152
Iona College, 48, 50
Israel, David, 115
Issel, Dan, 120

Jackson, Marie, 6, 57–59, *58*
Jackson, V. A., 6, 47, 57–59, *58, 63,* 97, 135
Jauss, Bill, 106
Jayhawks. *See* University of Kansas
Joe B. Hall Wildcat Lodge. *See* Wildcat Lodge
Johnson, Earvin "Magic," xvi, 2, 89, 93, *95,* 96, 158, 179n2
Johnson, Larry, xx, 10, *17,* 21, 143
Johnson, Walt, 16
Jones, Wallace "Wah Wah," 145, 157

Kansas State University, 140
Keightley, William "Bill," 16, 18, 69, 135, 155, 156–58, *157;* 1977–1978 season and, xvi, 26, 68, 69, 71–72, 79, 83, 96, 112, 120
Kemp, Joe, 47, 49
Kentucky's Conditioning Program for Basketball (Hall and Casey), 25
Kentucky state high school basketball tournament, 18
Kentucky Wildcats. *See* UK basketball; UK basketball 1977–1978 season; Wildcat fans
Kinney, John, *32,* 84
Kipling, Rudyard, 50

Laimbeer, Bill, 52
Leach, Tom, xix–xxi, 179n2.2
Ledford, Cawood, 10, 41, *72, 94*
Lee, Albert B., 38, 40
Lee, Butch, 89
Lee, James, *5, 13, 24, 39, 101, 119,* 132, 143, 152, 164; 1974–1975 season and, 13, 18–20; 1975–1976 season and, xiii, 1, 10, 174; 1975 NCAA Championship game and, xiii, xix, 1, 9, 10, 174; 1976–1977 season and, xiii, xix, 1, 2, 11–12, 141, 174; 1977–1978 season, early games and, 39, 42–43, 50; 1977–1978 season, later games and, 67, 79, 80, 84, 85, 86, 88; 1977–1978 season and, xiii, xiv–xv, 1, 5, 24, 25, 77, 138; 1977 NCAA Tournament regional finals and, xiii, xix, 1, 2, 12, 174; 1978 Final Four and, 101, 103; 1978 NCAA Championship game and, xiii, 111, 115, 117, 119, 120, 125, 128, 163, 174; 1978 NCAA Tournament play and, 91, 93; as freshman, 9, 10, 13, 18–20, 174; as leader for 1977–1978 season, xix–xx, 14–15, 16, 18, 22, 38, 86, 174; official practices, 28–29, 33, 37–38; qualifications and, 16, 18; quitting for an afternoon, xiv, 6, 38, 40; resolve to win and, 2, 5, 9, 12, 14
Leitsch, Bill, *32*
Lemons, Abe, 112
Lexington Center, 3
Lindenmeyer, John, 15
Louisiana State University (LSU), 118, 141, 181n7; UK basketball 1977–1978 season and, xiv, 67, 80–81, 82–83, 148, 162

Macklin, Durand, 67, 80
Macy, Kyle, *24, 82, 86, 104, 116;* 1976–1977 season and, xx, 12, 20–22, 52, 147; 1977–1978 season, early games and, 41–42, 43, 46, 50, 52; 1977–1978 season, later games and, 67, 72, 74, 79, 80, 82, 83, 84, 85, 86, 88; 1977–1978 season

Macy, Kyle *(cont.)*
    and, xiii, xiv, xv, xvii, xx, 1, 2, 12–13, 24, 40, 59, 77, 79, 147, 152, 154; 1978 Final Four and, 100, 104; 1978 NCAA Championship game and, xiii, 112, 114, 116, 117, 149, 164; 1978 NCAA Tournament play and, xvi, 91, 92, 93, 94–96; free-throw shooting, 1, 16, 52–53, 82, 94–96; pre-1978 NCAA Championship game and, 105–6, 107, 109, 111; preconditioning program, 15, 23–24, 25; qualifications, 3, 5, 12–13, 15, 16; redshirt year, xx, 12, 20–22, 52, 147
Maker's Mark commemorative bourbon, *139, 141*
Marquette University, 37, 89, 93, 182n1
McCombs, Walt, *24,* 31, *122*
McGill, John, 16
McGuire, Al, 112, 115
McGuire, Frank, 50
McKinney, Harold, xv
McLean, Gene, 128
Meeks, Jodie, 52
Memorial Coliseum, 137, 155; 1977–1978 season and, xvi, 39, 41–43, 61–62, 68, 71, 79, 148; 1978 NCAA Championship and, 129–30, 132; official practices, 4, 9, 13, 37
Memphis State University, 120
Mercer, Ron, 146

Miami University, 93, 182n4
Michigan State University, xvi, 89, 93–96, 158, 179n2
Minniefield, Dirk, 164
Mississippi State University, 17, 61, 72, 84–85, 141
Moncrief, Sidney, 102, *103,* 104–5, 148, 158, 183n3
"Mr. Basketball" titles, 3, 12, 30
"Mr. Wildcat." *See* Keightley, William "Bill"
Murphy, Mike, 7, 16, 24, 25, 26, 28, *32,* 33, 59, 60, 108, 155–59, *157*
Murphy, Zach, 157–58, *157*
"My Old Kentucky Home" (song, Foster), 132

Naismith, James, 46
Naismith Memorial Basketball Hall of Fame, 47
National Collegiate Athletic Association (NCAA): basketball, late 1970s and, xv, 2–3, 179n1, 179n3, 180–81n1. *See also* NCAA Championship game, 1978; NCAA Championships; NCAA Tournament; UK basketball; UK basketball 1977–1978 season
National Collegiate Athletic Association (NCAA) Division I. *See* NCAA Championships
National Collegiate Athletic Association (NCAA) Tournament. *See* NCAA Tournament

National Collegiate Basketball Hall of Fame, 148
National Hockey League, 102
National Invitational Tournament (NIT) 1976, xiii, 1, 10, 11, 174, 175, 176
NBA, 49, 82, 102, 140, 141, 144, 154, 183n3
NBC, 112, 115
NCAA Championship game, 1978, 6–7, 110, 111–23, 125, 126, 128, 143, 151–52, 181n1.2; Duke University and, 112–13, 115, 149, 162–64, 171, 174, 176; free throws and, 113, 115, 117, 120; Givens and, xiii–xiv, xx, 112, 113–14, 115–17, 120, 131, 149, 158, 162–64, 174; Hall and, xiii–xiv, xix, xx, 116, 117, 121, 149, 150; pregame, xix, 105–6, 107, 108–9, 111, 148–49, 158, 169–71. *See also other individual players, coaches, and managers*
NCAA Championships, 47; 1951 and, 28, 73, 140; 1966 and, xxi; 1975 and, xxi; 1977 and, 37; 1978 consolation matchups and, 109; 1979 and, 2, 179n2; 1996 and, xvii, 3; 1998 and, 3; 2012 and, xvii, 3; 2014 and, 144; Championship banner, *130;* Championship trophy and, 127, 158; scoring performances and, xx, 120. *See also* UK basketball; UK basketball 1974–1975 season; UK basketball 1977–1978 season
NCAA Men's Basketball Tournament Selection Committee (1978), 89
NCAA Tournament, 150, 179n1; 1976 and, 1, 10; 1977–1978 Atlantic Coast Conference Rookie of the Year, 113; 1977–1978 "Coach of the Year" and, 112; 1977 and, xiii, xix, 1, 2, 12, 174, 175, 176; 1978 National Coach of the Year and, 148; 1978 rankings and, 5–6, 37, 50, 89, 102, 111–12; 1978 Southeastern Conference (SEC) title and, 85, 147–48; Final Four and, 77, 102, 151. *See also* NCAA Championship game, 1978; NCAA Championships; UK basketball 1977–1978 season
Newton, Charles Martin "C. M.," 72–73, 74
Northern Kentucky University, 40, 41
Notre Dame University, 20, 89; 1978 Final Four and, xx, 105, 109, 113, 148, 149; UK basketball 1977–1978 season and, 41, 50, 52

Ole Miss, 67, 81–83, 181n7

Packer, Billy, 112
Pan American Games of 1975, 49
Parish, Robert, 49

Parsons, Dick, *11, 24*, 91, *92*, 137, 155; 1977–1978 season and, 1–2, 23, 24, 26, 43, 47, 53, 56–57, 75, 76; 1978 Final Four and, 100, 102, 103; 1978 NCAA Championship game and, 6–7, 105, 112, 120–21; official practices, 31, 34–35

Peck, Wiley, 85

Phillips, Mike, *5, 13, 17, 24,* 25, 60, *86, 92,* 137–38, 144; 1975–1976 season and, xiii, 1, 10, 17, 174; 1975 NCAA Championship game and, xiii, xix, 1, 10, 174; 1976–1977 season and, xiii, xix, 1, 2, 141, 174; 1977–1978 season, early games and, 46, 50; 1977–1978 season, later games and, 67, 79, 80, 85, 86, 88; 1977–1978 season and, xiii, xiv–xv, xix–xx, 2, 5, 24; 1977 NCAA Tournament regional finals and, xiii, xix, 1, 2, 12, 174; 1978 NCAA Championship game and, 112, 113, 120, 149, 163; 1978 NCAA Tournament play and, xvi, 91, 92, 93, 96; death, 135–36, 156; as freshman, xix, 9, 13, 18, 20, 152, 174; as leader for 1977–1978 season, xix–xx, 14–15, 16, 18, 22, 29, 86, 132, 174; pre-1978 NCAA Championship game, 105–6, 107; qualifications, xiv, 3, 16, 18; resolve to win, 2, 5, 9, 12, 14

Pitino, Rick, xvii, 3

Portland State University, 45, 50

potassium, 75–76

Purdue University, xiii, xx, 1, 12, 25

Ramsey, Derrick, 25

Ramsey, Frank, 28, 140–41, 157

Ramsey, Tripp, 28, 61–63, 100, *122,* 140–41, *142*

Razorbacks. *See* University of Arkansas

Rebeldome, 82, 181n7

RedHawks, 93, 182n4

Redskins, 93, 182n4

Regis College, 143

REO Speedwagon, 59

Ricke, Barbara, 56

Ridenour, Marla, 128

Robey, Rick, *5, 13, 24, 86–87, 92, 106, 110, 128,* 135; 1975–1976 season and, xiii, 1, 10, 174; 1975 NCAA Championship game and, xiii, xix, 1, 10, 174; 1976–1977 season and, xiii, 1, 2, 12, 141, 174; 1977–1978 season, early games and, 43, 44, 50; 1977–1978 season, later games and, 72, 74, 79, 80, 84, 85, 86, 87, 88; 1977–1978 season and, xiii, xvii, 5, 19–20, 24, 25, 33, 62, 68, 77; 1977 NCAA Tournament regional finals and, xiii, xix, 1, 2, 12, 174; 1978 Final Four and, 98,

102, 103, 105; 1978 NCAA Championship and, xiii, 128; 1978 NCAA Championship game and, 110, 112–13, 115, 116, 117, 118, 120, 149, 163; 1978 NCAA Tournament play and, xvi, 91, 93, 94; as freshman, xix, 9, 13, 18, 20, 49, 152, 174; as leader for 1977–1978 season, xix–xx, 12–13, 14–15, 16, 18, 22, 86, 132, 147, 174; pre-1978 NCAA Championship game, xx, 105–6, 149; pregame rituals, 44, 180n4; qualifications, xiv, 3, 16, 17, 18; resolve to win, 2, 4, 5, 9, 12–13, 14, 88; Wildcat fans and, xv–xvi, xviii

Ruland, Jeff, 50

Runnin' Rebels, 85–88, 158

Rupp, Adolph: illness and death of, 6, 44–47, 49–50; UK basketball and, 6, *11,* 24, 28, 43, 49–50, 73, 77, 117, 120, 128, 149, 157

Rupp Arena, 3, 62, 65, 68, 136, 145; 1977–1978 season, early games and, 21, 43, 44, 45; 1977–1978 season, later games and, xiv, xv, 67, 78, 82, 84; Senior Night, 85–88, *86,* 158

Sarbanes, Paul, 173, 175

"Season of No Celebration, The," xvii, xix, 4, 33–34, 105, 106, 112, 147–49, 152–53, 161–62

Seminoles, xvi, 34, 89–93

Shidler, Jay "The Blond Bomber," *24, 30,* 42–43, 105–6, *106,* 137–38, 156; 1977–1978 season and, 5, 13, 24, 44, 46, 59; 1978 Final Four and, 100, 102; 1978 NCAA Championship game and, 116, 117, 164; injury, 29, 31, 46; qualifications, xx, 3, 30, 74

Shively, Bernie, 52

Shively Memorial Plaque, 52

"Silk and Steel." *See* Givens, Jack "Goose"; Lee, James

Singletary, Otis, 81

Smith, G. J., *19*

Smith, Tony, 86

Smith, Tubby, 3, 157

Sosby, Tony, 26, 28, *32,* 60–61, 68, 82–83, 91, 126, *144*

Southeastern Conference (SEC), 67, 176; UK basketball 1978 title and, 85, 147–48

Southern Methodist University (SMU), 42, 43

South Korea, 145

Soviet National Team, *39,* 41–43

Spanarkel, Jim, 112

Spartans. *See* Michigan State University

Sports Illustrated, xx, 131

Stamper, Larry, 157

Stansbury, William, 132

Stephens, Tim, *24,* 47, *73,* 136, 137–38, 143; 1977–1978 season and, 22, 24, 26, 34, 50, 60, 73, 81; 1978 NCAA

Stephens, Tim *(cont.)*
  Championship and, 126–27, 140; 1978 NCAA Championship game and, 109, 117
Still, Art, 24
St. John's University, 50
"St. Louis and Five Smooth Stones," 108, 169–71
Sullivan, Don, 24, 32, 71, 122, 135, 142; 1977–1978 season and, 3, 24, 32, 43–44, 68, 81; Wildcat Lodge and, 56–57, 62
Sutton, Eddie, 102, 105, 183n2
Sycamores, 179n2
Syracuse University, 3

Tanner, Gary, 65, 66, 86
Tar Heels. *See* University of North Carolina (UNC)
Tarkanian, Jerry, 86, 88
Texas Christian University, 12
Theus, Reggie, 86, 88
"Three Basketeers." *See* Brewer, Ron; Delph, Marvin; Moncrief, Sidney
Tigers. *See* Auburn University; Louisiana State University (LSU)
Tkachenko, Vladimir, 39, 43
Tripucka, Kelly, 52
"Twin Towers." *See* Phillips, Mike; Robey, Rick

UCLA (University of California Los Angeles), 89, 120, 145; 1975 NCAA Championship game and, xix, 1, 9–10, 150
UK Athletics, 52, 132
UK basketball, 180n1, 180–81n1; 1951 NCAA Championship game and, 28, 73, 140; 1958–1959 season and, 24; 1970–1971 season and, 88; 1971–1972 season and, 11, 47; 1978–1980 seasons and, 52; 1980–1981 season and, 145; 1984–1985 season and, 183n2; 1996 NCAA Championship and, xvii, 3; 2007–2009 seasons and, 52; 2012–2013 season and, 56, 136; 2012 NCAA Championship and, xvii, 3; 2014–2015 season and, xvii, 156; 2015–2016 season, 21; African Americans and, 20, 143; all-time scoring list, 50, 70, 120; coaching staff and, 11, 20, 24, 34, 105, 117, 120, 183n2; expectations, 77, 120; field-goal percentage, 88; free-throw shooting, 52–53; legacy, xvii, xxi, 138–40; NCAA Championships and, xvii, xxi, 3, 4, 6, 47, 128, 144, 174; Adolph Rupp, 47, 49–50, 73, 77, 117, 120, 128, 149, 157; Southeastern Conference (SEC) titles, 85, 147–48, 176; student managers, 32, 153–54, 156–58; tradition, 144–46, 155–56, 175–76; UK Invitational Tournament, 50, 180n10; winning records, 11–12, 47
UK basketball 1974–1975 season, 18–19, 34; Final Four and, 98;

Indiana University and, xix, 152; NCAA Championship game and, xiii, xix, xxi, 1, 9–10, 150, 174, 175, 176; seniors as leaders, 19, 20
UK basketball 1975–1976 season, xiii, 1, 10, 11, 17, 61, 174, 175, 176
UK basketball 1976–1977 season, 11–12, 20–22, 141, 152; NCAA Tournament regional finals and, xiii, xix, 1, 2, 12, 174, 175, 176; Wildcat mascot and, 65, 66
UK basketball 1977–1978 season, 69, 70; Auburn and, 67, 80; coaching staff, 4, 5, 13, *24,* 28, 34, 53, 56–57, 61, 118, 137, 141, 143; commemoration and, 136, 139, 141, 157; depth of players, xiii–xviii, xx, 1, 27, 112; devotionals, 65–67, 107–9, 169–71, 181n1; early season games and, 6, 39, 41–46, 48, 49–52; expectations, 77, 79, 81, 106, 109, 119–20, 162; Final Four and, xvii, 7, 96, 97, 98–105, 123, 148–49, 151, 158, 179n1; first official team meeting, 4, 9, 13; Florida State University, xvi, 89–93; free-throw shooting and, 46, 52–53, 154; Indiana University and, 44; Iona College and, 48, 50; later season games and, xiv, 67, 72–74, 75, 78, 79–88, 148, 162, 181n7; legacy, 135–46, 149–50; losses, xiv, 72–74, 75, 79, 80–81, 82–83, 84, 148, 162; LSU and, xiv, 67, 80–81, 82–83, 148, 162; meals, 62–64, 65–67, 100; Miami University and, 93; Michigan State University and, xvi, 93–96, 158; Mississippi State University and, 72, 84–85; NCAA Championship and, xiii, xx–xxi, 3, 6, 7, 37, 122–23, 125–33, 143, 151, 173, 175, 176; NCAA Tournament play and, xvi, 89–96, 158; "no celebration" team, xvii, xix, 4, 33–34, 105, 106, 112, 147–49, 152–53, 161–62; Notre Dame University and, 41, 50, 52; official practices, 26–35, 37–38, 40, 147, 161; physicality of players, xiv–xv, 67, 74, 75–76, 112, 152; player qualifications, 3, 5, 12, 16, 17, 18, 30, 53; Portland State University and, 45, 50; preseason scrimmages, xv, 34, 35, 40–42, 156; ranking, 5–6, 37, 50, 89, 111–12; resolve to win, xix–xx, 2, 3–4, 5, 9, 12–14, 22, 35, 37, 91–92, 105, 140, 153, 162; seniors as leaders, xix–xx, 13–15, 16, 18–19, 22, 29, 33, 86, 96, 98–99, 118, 132, 147, 161, 174; shooting percentages, 1–2, 72, 83, 88, 154; snow and, xv, xvi, 67–69, 71; Southeastern

UK basketball 1977–1978 season *(cont.)*
    Conference (SEC) title and, 85, 147–48; Southern Methodist University (SMU) and, 42, 43; Soviet National Team and, *39,* 41–43; St. John's University and, 50; summer preconditioning program, 12, 14–15, 22, 23–26, 161; US Senate Resolution 427 and, 132–33, 173–76; University of Alabama and, 72–74, 75, 79, 84, 85, 148, 162; University of Arkansas and, 100–106, 112, 148, 158; University of Florida and, 67, 79; University of Georgia and, 78, 79, 85; University of Kansas and, 6, 44–46; University of Mississippi and, 67, 81–83, 181n7; University of Nevada Las Vegas (UNLV) and, 85–88, 158; University of South Carolina and, 49–50; University of Tennessee and, 82, 83–84, 85; Vanderbilt University and, 67, 88; Wildcat Lodge and, 6, 55–64, *56, 60,* 97, 129, 138, 153, 158; winning record, 5–6, 24, 121, 174. *See also* Hall, Joe B.; NCAA Championship game, 1978; Wildcat fans

UK basketball 1977–1978 season, student managers, 3, 7, 16, 24, 28, 32, 35, 43–44, 68, 82, 84, 125, 155, 156–57; reunions, 142, 144, 157; Wildcat Lodge and, 56–57, 60–61

UK football, 24–25, 65, 66, 176

UK Invitational Tournament, 50, 180n10

UK Radio Network, xiv, 4, 10, 41, 72, 179n2.2

"UK Wildcat Day in the city of Louisville," 132

University of Alabama, 55, 72–74, 75, 79, 144–45, 148, 162

University of Alabama football, 55, 144–45

University of Arkansas, 89, 100–106, 109, 112, 148, 158

University of Connecticut, 143–44

University of Florida, 67, 79

University of Georgia, 78, 79, 85

University of Houston, 89

University of Kansas, 3, 6, 44–46, 89

University of Kentucky. *See* UK basketball; UK basketball 1977–1978 season; Wildcat fans

University of Louisville, 9, 89

University of Memphis, 102

University of Michigan, 120

University of Mississippi, 67, 81–83, 181n7

University of Nevada Las Vegas (UNLV), 85–88, 158

University of North Carolina (UNC), xiii, xix, 1, 2, 12, 37, 89, 99

University of North Carolina (UNC) Charlotte, 1, 10

University of South Carolina, 49–50
University of Tennessee, 82, 83–84, 85
University of Texas, 112
University of the Cumberlands, 143
University of Utah, 3
University of Wisconsin, xvii
USA basketball team, 49, 184n1
US Senate Resolution 427, 132–33, 173–76

Valvano, Jim, 50
Vanderbilt University, 12, 67, 88
Vaught, Larry, xiii–xviii
Vesey, Kevin, *48*
Villanova University, 89
Volunteers, 82, 83–84, 85

Walker, Antoine, 145–46
Walker, Kenny, 120
Walton, Bill, 120
Warford, Reggie, 20, 143
Warriors, 37, 89, 93, 182n1
weight training, 23, 24–26, 149, 162
Western Kentucky University, 67
"When Earth's Last Picture Is Painted" (poem, Kipling), 50
Wildcat Coal Lodge, 44, 56, 137, 180n3
Wildcat fans, 21–22, 52, 138; 1977–1978 season and, 49–50, 79, 81, 96; 1978 NCAA Championship and, xx–xxi, 122–23, 125–33, 158, 164; cheerleaders and, 63, 65, 66; dedication, xv–xvi, xvii–xviii, xix, 64, 76–77, 127, 141, 143; preseason scrimmages, xv, 40–41, 156; Wildcat mascot and, 65, 66, 86
Wildcat Lodge, 6, 55–64, 97, 129, 138, 152, 153, 158, 180–81n1
Wildcats, Kentucky. *See* UK basketball
Wildcat Slush, 76, 181n1.2
"Wildcat Week," 132
Williams, LaVon, *24*, 71–72, *78*, 129, 137–38; 1977–1978 season and, 24, 31, 44, 60, 78, 81; 1978 NCAA Championship game and, 114, 116, 120, 143; 1978 NCAA Tournament play and, xvi, 91–92, 93; qualifications, xv, 3
"Wizard of Westwood." *See* Wooden, John
Wooden, John, xix, 9–10, 145
Woodson, Mike, 44
Woolridge, Orlando, 52

Year at the Top, A (McGill and Johnson), 16, 52